A·M·D·G

HELD In TRUST

2008 YEARS OF SACRED CULTURE

A catalogue of an exhibition
from the Stonyhurst College Collections,
held at St Francis Xavier's Church, Liverpool,
30 July–27 September 2008

Essays by
Michael Barnes SJ, Leo Gooch, J.A. Hilton,
Anthony Symondson SJ, Norman Tanner SJ, and Deborah Youngs,
with an Introduction by Thomas M. McCoog SJ
and
notes on exhibits
by Janet Graffius

Edited by
Maurice Whitehead

ST OMERS PRESS
Stonyhurst
MMVIII

First published in 2008 by
St Omers Press Ltd
3-9 Cripps Road, Cirencester, Gloucestershire GL7 1HN
www.stomerspress.co.uk

CIP data for this title are available from the British Library

ISBN 978-0-9553592-3-1

Designed by Kaleidoscope ADM Ltd, Liverpool
Printed in Singapore by Imago Publishing Ltd

Front cover illustration:
Portrait of Pope Gregory the Great (*circa* 540-604) from Stonyhurst Ms VII, f.3r.
The manuscript was completed at St Alban's Abbey in Hertfordshire between 1167 and 1183.

Back cover illustration:
Monogram of the Society of Jesus from an edition of the *Exercitia Spiritualia*, or *Spiritual Exercises* of St Ignatius Loyola, published at the press of the English Jesuit college at St Omers in 1610.
IHS are the first letters in Greek of the name *Jesus*.

Contents

Editor's Preface

On 21 January 1840, a group of nine lay Catholics, all of them local businessmen, met at the *Rose and Crown* tavern in Cheapside, Liverpool, to form themselves into "a provisional committee for the formation of a society with the view to erect a Catholic church in Liverpool to be presented to the President of Stonyhurst College".

Some of the nine had received their education at the hands of members of the Society of Jesus, generally known as the Jesuits, at Stonyhurst College in Lancashire. All of them were determined to help realise a dream that had been the aspiration of the Society of Jesus — the largest religious order in the Roman Catholic Church, devoted to missionary and educational work — since the arrival of the first Jesuits in England and Wales in 1580. This was to create, in an urban setting in an English town or city, a Jesuit *collegium*.

The Latin word in this context means considerably more than the English word *college*: it denotes a church, with outreach into the community, and a school for boys, all under a rector whose duty it is, according to the Jesuit *Constitutions*, to preside over and guide the combined missionary, educational and cultural enterprise. Liverpool, which was rapidly becoming one of the largest ports in the British empire by the early 1840s, was the location chosen for this pioneering venture.

From shortly after the foundation of the Society of Jesus in 1540 by Ignatius Loyola (*circa* 1492-1556), Jesuit colleges had sprung up by popular demand in towns and cities all over continental Europe. Municipalities wishing to enjoy the educational and cultural benefits offered by a Jesuit school were expected to provide the necessary buildings, while the *Constitutions* of the Society of Jesus demanded that Jesuits offered their services as teachers and educators without charge.

By 1760, across the world from Paraguay to India, there were seven hundred and twenty-eight such Jesuit colleges, mostly comprising day schools, many of them in Europe with 1,500 to 2,000 pupils, and with churches attached to them open to the public. In certain places, Jesuit schools were open to all male students, whether or not they were Catholic: by this time, certain female religious orders had taken up many of the educational ideas of the Jesuits and were applying them to the education of girls. All of these institutions became important places of religion, education and culture.

Within Jesuit colleges, educational and cultural emphases on public speaking, debating, drama, music and literary studies played a formative role in the subsequent careers of a host of European men of letters: Calderón, Corneille, Goldoni, Molière, Racine, Tasso and Voltaire, and, in more recent times, Arthur Conan Doyle and James Joyce, the film directors, Luis Buñuel, Alfred Hitchcock and Louis Malle, and the actor, Charles Laughton, all received a Jesuit education. Equally, the Jesuits' encouragement of scholarship in mathematics and the sciences, particularly in higher education, helped foster the outstanding talent of students such as René Descartes (1596-1650), often regarded as the father of modern philosophy; the Italian mathematician and physicist, Evangelista Torricelli (1608-1647), who invented the barometer; and the Moravian Jesuit botanist, Brother Georg Josef Kamel (1661-1706), whose memory is preserved in the name of the *camellia* flower. Early scholastic successes of this type helped earn the Jesuits a formidable reputation as the "schoolmasters of Europe".

Jesuit colleges across Europe soon built up important collections of artefacts, both sacred and secular, to aid the teaching of a wide-ranging curriculum and to provide deeper understanding of Catholic belief. Many colleges attracted bequests from former students grateful for the education they had received. Some of these *alumni* ranged far and wide in their travels, bringing back with them remarkable and precious objects, not all of them sacred. In an age predating public museums and encyclopaedias, Jesuit colleges began to develop their own *cabinets of curiosities* – or prototype museums – better to help both their students and the wider public understand the world, both sacred and secular, around them. The most famous of these was the cabinet of curiosities created at the Roman College of the Society of Jesus by the distinguished Jesuit scientist, Father Athanasius Kircher (1601-1680): his collection developed into the *Museum Kircherianum* in Rome, probably the earliest public museum in the world in 1651.

For political reasons, such developments were totally impossible in post-Reformation England and Wales. From the reign of Elizabeth I until the late eighteenth century, a series of penal laws prohibited Catholics from operating their own churches or schools. As a result, the missionary work of the Jesuits in the two countries had to be conducted clandestinely, mainly through the attachment of Jesuit chaplains to the households of the Catholic gentry. In south-west Lancashire, families such as the Blundells of Crosby, the Molyneux of Sefton and the Scarisbricks of Scarisbrick sheltered Jesuit chaplains, while neighbouring Catholic gentry families such as the Harringtons of Aigburth Hall and the Norrises of Speke concealed as domestic chaplains within their households Benedictines or members of the secular clergy – most of them, like their Jesuit counterparts, educated in continental European colleges and seminaries.

Unable to operate schools officially at home, the English Jesuits opened their first college at Saint-Omer in the Spanish Netherlands in 1593. This school was, of necessity, a boarding establishment, rather than the more usual Jesuit day school found in continental Europe towns and cities. The English Jesuit college at Saint-Omer soon became better known by its abbreviated, anglicised name – *St Omers*. Between 1593 and 1762, despite English laws prohibiting the education of Catholics in Catholic schools outside the kingdom, at least four thousand boys, mainly from England, Wales and Ireland, as well as from English settlements in the Caribbean and from Maryland (where the English Jesuits had a number of mission stations) received their education at St Omers. Significant numbers of them travelled from Lancashire for their education: despite the distance, danger and expense involved, many of the leading Catholic families from the Liverpool area entrusted the education of their sons to the Jesuits at St Omers.

In 1762, when the Jesuits were expelled from France (Saint-Omer by then lying in French territory), the members of St Omers College had to flee across the border into the Austrian Netherlands. There, they re-established themselves in Bruges, having taken with them what sacred treasures they could salvage quickly.

Eleven years later, in 1773, when the Society of Jesus was suppressed universally for political reasons by the papacy, the English

Jesuits and their scholars had to flee again. This time they escaped into the tiny independent principality of Liège, where a tolerant prince-bishop allowed them to continue their educational activity in the former English Jesuit college of philosophy and theology which had been founded in 1624 in the city of Liège. There St Omers continued its twice-transplanted existence as the *Académie anglaise* or English Academy, again sheltering as many of the sacred treasures as the now suppressed Jesuits and their pupils had managed to salvage and safeguard in the confusion of the times.

When, in 1794, French revolutionary troops advanced on Liège, the suppressed English Jesuits and their pupils had to make a hurried escape for a third time – this time to Lancashire. A former Bruges student of the English Jesuits, Thomas Weld (1750-1810), of Lulworth Castle in Dorset, a substantial landowner, offered the academic refugees from Liège a home in his dilapidated and largely uninhabited family seat in Lancashire, Stonyhurst Hall, near Clitheroe. When the Society of Jesus was restored in England and Wales in 1803 by the papacy, Stonyhurst became for many years the headquarters of the English Jesuits. As English law now allowed Catholics to operate their own schools, the college at Stonyhurst began to flourish – and to spawn new day schools in the wider, international Jesuit tradition.

A beginning in this direction was made in 1842 with the opening of St Francis Xavier's day school in Liverpool. The neighbouring church of St Francis Xavier was opened in 1848. This was duly presented by the lay committee, formed at the *Rose and Crown* in Liverpool in 1840, to the president of Stonyhurst College, who was also the provincial superior of the English Jesuits. The church was thereby handed over to the missionary care of the Jesuit fathers and brothers who continue their work down to the present day. In 1851, following a visit to Liverpool by the Dutch superior general of the Society of Jesus, Father Jan Philip Roothaan (1785-1853), the fast-developing Liverpool school and church were raised, in the Jesuit tradition, to the status of a fully fledged *collegium* – the *Collegium Sancti Francisci Xaverii* – or St Francis Xavier's College.

By 1900, St Francis Xavier's College and parish, with its associated elementary schools, was the largest Jesuit missionary and educational enterprise in Britain, with over 2,500 pupils and almost 11,000 parishioners, served by a community of twenty-five Jesuits. In size and scope, the Jesuit religious, educational and cultural enterprise in Liverpool now matched any of the great Jesuit colleges to be found in continental European cities such as Paris, Lyon or Brussels. Though St Francis Xavier's College was relocated to Woolton, in the suburbs of Liverpool, in 1961, its large collegiate building of 1876, adjacent to St Francis Xavier's Church, and now occupied by Liverpool Hope University, stands as a reminder of the scale on which the Jesuit educational enterprise in Liverpool was conceived.

The unbroken survival of St Omers College as a Jesuit institution from its beginnings in 1593 to its present-day manifestation as Stonyhurst College, despite three major international transplantations, is unique in European educational and cultural history. Even more remarkable is the fact that so many precious, sacred artefacts entrusted to the English Jesuits both at home and abroad over the centuries have survived, despite momentous religious upheavals in England and Wales between the sixteenth and eighteenth centuries, two serious fires at St Omers in 1684 and 1725, and the turmoil and disasters of 1762, 1773 and 1794 at St Omers, Bruges and Liège.

The international Jesuit tradition of collecting and preserving precious sacred artefacts, held in trust and preserved for the benefit of posterity, is a long one. Begun generally more than 450 years ago, and, in an English Jesuit context, started at St Omers in 1593, that tradition has continued at Stonyhurst since 1794, at St Francis Xavier's in Liverpool since the early 1840s, and continues down to the present day. Some of the items held in trust by the present-day British Province of the Society of Jesus are well known internationally – such as the seventh-century Anglo-Saxon St Cuthbert Gospel of St John, also known as the *Stonyhurst Gospel*, now on loan to the British Library in London where it is on permanent display; and the late-fourteenth-century triptych, known as the *Mary, Queen of Scots Triptych*, from Campion Hall, Oxford, on loan to the Victoria and Albert Museum. Other artefacts held in trust today by the British Jesuits and by Stonyhurst College are less well known – and it is a selection of these that forms the basis of the exhibition, *Held in Trust: 2008 Years of Sacred Culture*.

In the Introduction to this booklet, Father Thomas McCoog explains the religious and cultural *significance* of what has been preserved through the centuries and is now displayed in this exhibition, with many of the objects on view to the general public for the first time.

Thereafter, six experts on the five main periods of history and one broader theme represented in the exhibition provide a general introduction to help place into a wider context the exhibits relating to their area of expertise.

After each section, Janet Graffius, curator of the collections at Stonyhurst College, provides detailed notes on each of the exhibits. Unless otherwise indicated, the articles on display are from the Stonyhurst collections. Vestments and church plate from the collections of St Francis Xavier's Church, Liverpool, displayed during this exhibition near the altars of the church, are not included in this catalogue.

Some of the artefacts in this exhibition would certainly have been familiar to members of the group of men who gathered at the *Rose and Crown* in Liverpool in 1840 to make better known the missionary, educational and cultural work of the Jesuits. All of the artefacts form part of our common national, European and world heritage, whatever our personal beliefs may be.

May their public display in this exhibition be a fitting contribution to Liverpool's status as European Capital of Culture, 2008.

Maurice Whitehead
Department of History
Swansea University

St David's Day, 1 March 2008

5

Acknowledgements

The exhibition, *Held in Trust: 2008 Years of Sacred Culture*, has been planned over a period of three years by an organising committee which has met regularly at St Francis Xavier's Church, Liverpool.

The committee – David Brazendale, Theresa Doyle, Mike Edwards, Peter Furmedge, Janet Graffius, Michael O'Connell, Debbie Reynolds, Joseph Sharples, John Tiernan and Maurice Whitehead – has been chaired throughout by Brother Kenneth Vance SJ, whose infectious enthusiasm and unflagging energies have sparked the imagination and drawn out the individual talents of all its members in a large team enterprise.

Thanks are due first and foremost to Janet Graffius for providing notes on the exhibits and for undertaking the large task of organising the exhibition as a whole.

Special thanks are due to National Museums Liverpool for the loan of display cabinets; to Michael Barnes SJ, Leo Gooch, J. A. Hilton, Thomas M. McCoog SJ, Anthony Symondson SJ, Norman Tanner SJ, and Deborah Youngs for providing introductory essays to the catalogue; to Professor John France, Neil Griffiths, Professor Gareth Elwyn Jones, Ricardo Koza, Thomas M. McCoog SJ and Christopher Whitehead for commenting on early drafts of the catalogue; and to Joseph Sharples for providing notes on Pugin; to Brother James Hodkinson SJ, assistant archivist of the British Province of the Society of Jesus in London, for help with archival references; to Mike Edwards, Mike Danher, Ken Ashcroft and the rest of the design team at Kaleidoscope ADM Ltd, of Liverpool, for their help, patience and care; and to Anthony Eyre of St Omers Press for seeing the publication to completion.

The essay contributed by Norman Tanner SJ first appeared in *The Church Times* (www.churchtimes.co.uk). The Liverpool Record Office, Liverpool Libraries, Stonyhurst College and the Trustees of the British Province of the Society of Jesus own the copyright of the images reproduced in this catalogue by their kind permission.

Finally, a debt of gratitude is due to the headmaster and governors of Stonyhurst College and to the British Province of the Society of Jesus for agreeing to loan many of the exhibits; and to the congregation of St Francis Xavier's, Liverpool, both for hosting this exhibition and for providing the volunteers to allow public access to it in the context of Liverpool's status as European Capital of Culture, 2008.

Introduction

THOMAS M. McCOOG SJ

From stamps to autographs; from bottle tops to empty tins; from postcards to military insignia; from thimbles to keys: anything and everything is collectible. A cursory visit to *eBay* reveals the present-day extent and diversity of collecting. Many comment how a hobby can become an obsession, but few offer any explanation. Philipp Blom studied the "urge to collect" in *To Have and To Hold: An Intimate History of Collectors and Collecting* (London, 2002). Blom conducts the reader on a tour from Renaissance cabinets of curiosities to unpacked crates of art, sculpture and architecture purchased by American moguls, memorably filmed in *Citizen Kane*.

What confers value upon a collected object? Why, asks Blom, "is someone prepared to pay a small fortune for a stamp that is no longer valid, for an empty matchbox that missed the rubbish bin only because its last user had a poor aim, for a bottle that has not contained any wine for decades?" (p.166). The author argues that their value lies in their *significance*: "they mean something, stand for something, carry associations that make them valuable in the eye of the collector".

"Where was your church before Luther?", Catholics across continental Europe demanded of sixteenth-century Protestants. If the reformed Church is the Church established by Jesus Christ, where was it before the publication of Martin Luther's 95 theses in 1517? Jesus promised that his Spirit would remain in the Church and guide it. So where was this Church during the 1500 years prior to Luther's protest? Were Luther's antecedents patristic and medieval heretics? Did the reformed Church suddenly appear out of nowhere? How could the Church, under divine guidance, have been so wrong for so long?

In England the situation was different. In the reformations initiated by Henry VIII, his son Edward VI, and daughter Elizabeth I, the English Church claimed to be the legitimate descendant of Christianity as established within the kingdom, perhaps by Joseph of Arimathea, before a later introduction of Roman corruption and abuses. Crown officials such as Thomas Cromwell purged colleges, cathedrals, and churches of any manuscript or work of art considered superstitious or "smacking of popery". Chantries were destroyed, tombs looted, statues maimed, parchments burned and paintings whitewashed. Catholics loyal to the old religion watched in horror as their devotional and religious patrimony was destroyed, and their churches and cathedrals occupied by ecclesiastics loyal to the reform. Prosperous monasteries and abbeys, once institutions integral to England's social fabric, became now Shakespeare's famous "Bare ruin'd choirs where late the sweet birds sang".

In possession of titles and properties, the reformers portrayed themselves as restorers of the pristine glory of the English Church, now finally cleansed of contamination after centuries of subservience to Roman control. If English Catholics dared ask the reformers where their Church was before Luther, the said reformers could simply point to the churches and cathedrals currently used for their worship. Possession of the traditional places of worship demonstrated, more clearly and forcefully than any theological argument, Protestant claims of historical continuity with England's religious past.

English Catholics were disenfranchised intruders. In the ensuing theological and historical publications, Catholic controversialists, historians and antiquarians refuted Protestant claims that their Church was the legitimate continuation of England's past. Left without the buildings, English Catholics claimed as their own, discarded items of England's Christian past. As reformers defaced England's Christian heritage, Catholics saved what they could from the looted tombs and the suppressed abbeys. They cherished what the reformers despised.

The objects in this exhibition truly have *significance*. As the medieval Church gave way to the Reformation, English Catholics, often unnamed, collected devotional, pious, and liturgical objects, often at considerable danger to themselves. Some, such as the alabaster panel of the adoration of the Magi and the Lucca chasuble, they hid away, perhaps in hope that a better day would dawn. Other objects, such as the St Dunstan and Henry VII chasubles, Cardinal Wolsey's Book of Hours, and the Aragon Mass vestments, were entrusted to continental institutions such as the English Jesuit colleges at St Omers or Liège for preservation for future generations. English Catholics collected religious items with significance extending far beyond the borders of their kingdom – for example, the relic of the Holy Thorn with its associations with the crusades, the Sainte-Chapelle in Paris, and Mary, Queen of Scots.

Arguably the most treasured objects are those associated with the survival of Catholicism during the approximately three hundred years of legal proscription. Persecution varied depending on time and place, but the anti-Catholic laws remained ever a threat. Anyone not complying with the religious statutes risked everything. Liturgical items were hidden in trunks to avoid detection. Martyrs, such as Sir Thomas More, Edmund Campion, and Edward Oldcorne, were many and their relics cherished.

The accession of James II in 1685 seemed to be an answer to the prayers of English and Welsh Catholics. They would no longer have to worship in embassy chapels, or behind locked, closed doors. Three years later, in 1688, the so-called Glorious Revolution ended their respite but not their hopes. Catholics did not abandon the House of Stuart, and many flirted with Jacobitism as they sought to replace the Hanoverian dynasty with the legitimate Stuarts.

In the late eighteenth century, Parliament began to enact legislation that lifted many of the financial and penal burdens carried by English and Welsh Catholics. The Catholic Relief Act of 1829 removed most of the remaining disabilities. Catholics celebrated their freedom, and reclaimed their heritage, with the construction of numerous churches and cathedrals in the different styles of the Gothic Revival. During this "second spring" Catholicism once again became a prominent feature on the English landscape.

English and Welsh Catholics did not simply look backwards with a *world that we have lost* simplicity to better times. They honoured their past and hoped to transmit it to the future. But even during the most difficult times, they were also well aware of Catholic missionaries in the new, unknown parts of the globe, and artistic, spiritual developments in Catholic Europe. Catholic culture blossomed in continental Europe; Catholic missionaries disseminated the Gospel throughout the globe. Most likely the first Englishman to visit India was the Jesuit, Thomas Stephens, in 1579. Reports of the success of such missionaries, translated and published, consoled and encouraged persecuted English and Welsh Catholics. A desire for religious freedom even prompted some English Catholics to embark for the New World and establish the colony of Maryland in 1633. New worlds; exotic worlds; worlds to convert; worlds to study. Worlds that slowly and sometimes painfully opened European eyes to "God's grandeur".

eam. Signum est domus isra

Explicit prima pars ezechiel

prophe. Incipit epla beati Gre

ii pape ad marinianum epm

Dilectissimo fri Marinia

epo. Gregorius seruu

seruoꝛ dei. Omelia

que in beatum Ezechiel ppha

ita ut coram poplo loquebar

cepte sunt; multis curis irrue

ab; inabolitione reliqueꝛã. S

Crying 'God for Harry! England and St George!

NORMAN TANNER SJ

Throughout the four centuries before the Reformation, England was part of Western Christendom, and this was a basic framework for the Church of England.

In 1054, less than half a century earlier, the schism between the Eastern and Western Churches began with the mutual excommunications of the bishops of Constantinople and Rome. At the time, and for long after, most people assumed the schism would soon be healed, but, sadly, it has endured to this day. Soon after the end of our period, the Reformation began, producing divisions within the Western Church itself.

By Europe is meant here western and parts of central Europe. England's relations with Europe during this long time can be looked at in various ways. Two extremes, however, must be avoided.

On the one hand, it is wrong to see the English Church as simply a province of the Western Church with virtually no self-identity or autonomy or initiative of its own: as if England were merely reproducing, for the most part at a weaker level, what was going on elsewhere in Europe. This is a simplistic view, suggested by some Roman Catholic scholars of an earlier generation, mostly from continental Europe and not themselves English, which does no justice to the brilliance and creativity of the English Church in this period.

The other extreme is to suggest that the English Church was already virtually a national Church, going its own way and almost independent of the rest of Western Christendom.

Relations with the papacy

The English Church's relations with the papacy may seem the obvious place to begin a study of England's place in Western Christendom. We shall start here, but with some hesitation. We have to be careful not to exaggerate the importance of the papacy at this time, nor to project the preoccupations of the Reformation and later periods back into the Middle Ages. Most people, for example, would probably have had little idea of the name of the pope of the time, and no "picture" of him such as has been possible since the arrival of television and other mass media.

On the one hand, the tensions can be highlighted. Just before the beginning of the period, William the Conqueror (1027/8–1087) was king, and Lanfranc (*circa* 1010–1089) was Archbishop of

Canterbury. Both were devout men, who worked closely together, and while they supported many of the aims of the reforming papacy of the time, they strongly resisted those that seemed to encroach on the rights of the king in his government of the realm and of the Church.

Later, in the fourteenth century, when the papacy moved from Rome to Avignon in southern France, and when all the popes for some seventy years, 1307–1378, were Frenchmen, there was tension between England and what was seen as a "French papacy", especially because for most of the time England was at war with France, in the Hundred Years War, and the popes were seen as favouring France in this quarrel.

On the other hand, Nicholas Breakspear (*d.* 1159) of St Albans in Hertfordshire was elected pope as Hadrian IV in 1154. He was an able pope, whose reign was cut short by an early death. There seemed nothing unusual in electing an Englishman to the post, though in fact he was to be the only man from the British Isles ever to become pope.

Later, too, during the papal schism of 1378 to 1417 – when there were two claimants, and sometimes three, to the papacy – England was a strong supporter of the "Roman" pope against the Francophile claimant based in Avignon. And afterwards the English government was seen as an important ally of the popes in their struggles with a succession of church Councils about authority in the Church.

Canon law

Historians have debated how far the law of the Church of England was already in the Middle Ages independent of the canon law of the Church of Rome. Frederick Maitland and William Stubbs began the debate in the late nineteenth century. Stubbs argued for a large measure of autonomy pointing especially to the book on canon law entitled *Provinciale,* which was written by the Englishman William Lyndwood (*circa* 1375–1446), in the fifteenth century, and which seemed to Stubbs to prove an independent tradition of English canon law. Maitland, on the other hand, argued that *Provinciale* always pre-supposed the binding force of *Corpus Iuris Canonici,* the canon law of Western Christendom as a whole, and that English canon law was merely a set of by-laws or appendices to the basic law.

Maitland had the better of the argument, and his basic thesis about the recognition of *Corpus Iuris Canonici* in England provided to be right. On the other hand, he interpreted canon law in an overly legal or literal sense, as if it were a code, somewhat similar to the Napoleonic Code of a later period. Hence, Stubbs's emphases on custom, and on a certain flexibility within the *Corpus,* so that it was open to a good measure of interpretation and adaptation within the English scene, were important insights, too.

The English Church was, for the most part, well able to manage its own affairs, and unwelcome interventions from outside were the exception, not the rule. This self-sufficiency in church law, as in other areas of church life, became more pronounced in the late Middle Ages, in the fourteenth and fifteenth centuries.

Continental Councils

Councils provide another example of England's relations with Western Christendom. Ecumenical Councils, such as Nicaea I and Chalcedon and others in the early Church, were regarded as impossible without the participation of the Eastern Church, so that *General Councils* were the highest and most authoritative church Councils in the medieval West. They were the European Parliament of the time.

Ten of them were held in various cities of Europe between 1123 and 1512-17: the five Lateran Councils in Rome, two in Lyons and one in Vienne in France, one in Constance in Germany, and one which began in Basel in Switzerland and ended in Florence in Italy.

There were representatives from the British Isles at almost all these General Councils, and – another sign of interest – some of the best contemporary accounts of their proceedings were written by English chroniclers. English bishops were particularly zealous in enforcing in their dioceses the decrees of the Fourth Lateran Council of 1215, which was the most thoroughgoing of the ten Councils with regard to reform of the Church.

On the other hand, English bishops were ready to defend the interests of their country when the occasion demanded, as happened more notably at the Council of Constance.

Theology and learning

The British Isles played a full part in the development of Western theology. Anselm of Canterbury (*circa* 1033–1109) was the most brilliant mind of his age. He is often called the first *scholastic,* inasmuch as he was the first medieval theologian to question the Christian religion systematically by reason, though he put it more gently in his famous description of theology as "faith seeking understanding" *(fides quaerens intellectum).* He proposed a proof of the existence of God, the *ontological argument* that still excites philosophers today.

Anselm spent the last part of his life in England, as Archbishop of Canterbury from 1093 until his death in 1109, yet he was a cosmopolitan European. He was born and brought up in Aosta in northern Italy and he spent many years as a monk at Bec in northern France: so that while he is known here as Anselm of Canterbury, in Italy he is known as Anselm of Aosta, and in France as Anselm of Bec.

John Duns Scotus (*circa* 1266–1308) and William of Ockham (*circa* 1285–1347) were also the leading thinkers of their time, and they, too, were European figures. The former, as his name indicates, was born in Scotland, possibly in the town of Duns: he became a Franciscan friar, and taught at both Oxford and Paris Universities, and at Cologne in Germany. Whereas Thomas Aquinas (1224/5-1274), his brilliant predecessor, had emphasised knowledge and reason, Scotus stressed more the importance of the will and of love.

William of Ockham, from Ockham in Surrey, where his shrine exists today in the parish church, also became a Franciscan friar and taught at both Oxford and Paris. During a second spell of teaching in Oxford, he ran into trouble with the chancellor of the university on account of his teaching, and as a result he was summoned to appear before the pope in Avignon.

He obeyed the summons, but, having spent some time in Avignon, and fearing the punishment that might befall him, he fled to Germany and spent the last twenty years of his life in Bavaria under the protection of Emperor Louis. At Oxford and Paris, Ockham wrote on philosophy and theology; in Germany, on political theory.

Ockham was a highly original thinker: his sharp mind gained the epithet *Ockham's razor*. Analytical and critical, more positively, however, he strove to preserve the transcendence and freedom of God from any attempt to tie God down to our human categories and wishes: a Barthian before Karl Barth (1886-1968). He was the most influential thinker in Western Christendom, especially in university and academic circles, during the two centuries before the Reformation, more influential even than Aquinas or Scotus.

Riches of art

The cathedrals, so well kept by the Church of England today, are the architectural glories of medieval England. The thousands of medieval parish churches that still survive are beautiful and fascinating, often exquisitely so, at a more intimate level.

At both levels, the architecture was influenced by developments on the Continent, Norman in the early period and Gothic later. Even so, the rich variety and distinctive local characteristics are obvious to any visitor. In England, particularly, there developed a national style in the later Middle Ages: English Perpendicular or Late English Gothic.

Much the same may be said of other aspects of the Church of England's artistic heritage from the Middle Ages, though this is often difficult to know for certain, because much religious art was destroyed after the Reformation.

There is the fine stained glass in York Minister, for example; or the murals in Chaldon Parish Church in Surrey, showing even Byzantine influences; or the Wilton diptych that portrays King Richard II before Mary, the saints and angels; or the five-panel retable now in Norwich Cathedral, depicting Christ's Passion, death and resurrection, seemingly a mixture of English and Flemish influences; or the twelfth-century ivory cross or the fourteenth- or fifteenth-century travelling-altar in gold and enamel, preserved respectively in the Cloisters Museum in New York, and in the Victoria and Albert Museum, as the Campion Hall triptych, in London.

Popular religion

The English Church was a community of remarkable energy and variety, especially in view of the much smaller population: just a tenth of what it is today, and with the large majority living in the countryside.

For many people, a primary identity in religion, as in other matters was the locality: the village and the parish in the countryside, the parish or a street or a ward in the towns. In larger towns, such as Norwich or York, there could be as many as fifty parish churches; in London, much the largest city with perhaps 40,000 inhabitants in 1300, there were more than one hundred.

Guilds and confraternities, sometimes based on crafts and trades, sometimes on parish churches or religious houses, provided another identity for many people, especially in towns, providing a mixture of religious, social and economic functions and activities, including the drama of the mystery plays.

The diocese, with its bishop and cathedral (sometimes two), was another unit: seventeen in England, five in Wales, separate hierarchies in Scotland and Ireland. But the diocese was largely an administrative unit. An area with which more people probably identified was the region: sometimes this coincided with a diocese. In some ways England was still a federation of regions, the Church of England a federation of regional churches: the north with its capital of York, East Anglia with Norwich, the Midlands, the West Country, the south-east with the national capital of London.

There were the liturgical rites of the regions: the Norwich rite, the Hereford rite, and the expanding Sarum (or Salisbury) rite. There also seem to have been noticeable regional variations in religious temperament, especially in the later Middle Ages: a more "high-church", almost baroque, Christianity in East Anglia and the diocese of York; a more puritanical spirit in the south-east and the Midlands, with large Lollard communities in London, Coventry and Leicester.

At the popular level, too, it is remarkable how much Christians from the British Isles took an interest in the wider fortunes of Christianity. The crusades, however much we may now regret them as a false goal, were one aspect of this wider concern.

Pilgrimages abroad were another popular activity. There was a hostel in Rome, still surviving today as the English College, which was specifically for English pilgrims in the city. Margery Kempe (*circa* 1373-*circa* 1438), the redoubtable lady from King's Lynn in Norfolk, after she had borne fourteen children, set out on a series of distant pilgrimages: to Jerusalem and Rome in 1413–15, to Santiago de Compostela in Spain in 1417–18, and to Norway, to Danzig in Prussia and back through Paris in 1434–5, when she was probably aged at least sixty.

1.1

BOOK OF HOMILIES OF POPE GREGORY THE GREAT

Stonyhurst Ms VII

Vellum, ink, pigment and gold leaf, 360 x 560mm

Circa **1167-1183**

Pope Gregory (*circa* 540-604) was elected to the papacy in 590 and made his mark as a tireless champion of organisation and charity. He was one of the four great Latin Fathers of the Church, and his writings were widely distributed and read from the seventh century onwards. He was responsible for reform of the Roman liturgy and for the plain chant known today as *Gregorian chant*.

Gregory had a particular calling to the Anglo-Saxon peoples of the British Isles, popularly supposed to have been sparked when he saw blue-eyed, blond-haired slave boys in Rome and asked who they were. On being told that they were Angles, he was reported by the Venerable Bede to have replied that they were *Non Anglii, sed Angeli – Not Angles, but angels.*

Shortly after this episode, when he was still an abbot, he wished to leave Rome and undertake missionary work in Britain, but was prevented by popular outcry from abandoning his monastic community. When he was elected to the papacy he commissioned St Augustine to travel to Kent and convert the people to Christianity. For this he was known fondly as *Gregorius noster,* or *our Gregory,* in England throughout the Middle Ages.

The Book of Homilies on the Prophet Ezekiel is a series of twenty-two sermons delivered by Gregory, many of which touch on the nature of prophecy. There is a popular story that these homilies were dictated to Gregory by a dove which whispered in his ear, indicating that they were divinely inspired. Gregory is usually shown in paintings or illustrations with a bishop's crosier and a dove.

This particular manuscript dates from the late twelfth century. There is an inscription at the head of the first page which informs the reader that the book was written by the hand of Simon, the abbot of St Albans in Hertfordshire, and warning of a dreadful fate which would befall anyone unworthy enough to steal the book. Simon was abbot between 1167 and 1183, and, apart from his reputation as a fine and clear calligrapher, he was also a close friend of St Thomas of Canterbury, popularly known as Thomas Becket.

The illumination shown here depicts Pope Gregory holding his Book of Homilies and sitting inside an initial letter *D.* The artist has wittily drawn Gregory disseminating the text from the book he holds out into the surrounding page. The face is so particular and so individual that it is very likely to be that of Abbot Simon himself: the custom of including within an illuminated manuscript a portrait of the person commissioning it was a not uncommon practice in the Middle Ages.

There is no information as to how this manuscript reached Stonyhurst College. It is probable that, like so many other sacred manuscripts, it was hidden during the Reformation and given to the College either during its time on the continent or in the nineteenth century when it settled at its present site in Lancashire.

1.2

YORK MISSAL FROM TATHAM, LANCASHIRE
Stonyhurst Ms III
Vellum, ink, pigment and gold leaf, 365 x 272 mm
Fourteenth century

A missal is a book containing all the prayers said by a Catholic priest at the altar while he is celebrating Mass. The order of the Mass varies from day to day as different feasts and solemnities are celebrated, and the missal contains all the variations for the liturgical year. This missal is in Latin, as all Masses were celebrated in Latin until 1964 when the vernacular language of each country was allowed to be used in the liturgy, following changes brought about by the Second Vatican Council (1962-1965).

Before the thirteenth century, missals varied widely from region to region, but from about 1250 onwards they began to conform to a single, more standardised, type. Each diocese had the freedom to order the inclusion of different prayers and different saints' feast days, according to local tradition.

In England the first and most influential of these diocesan variations was laid down by the Bishop of Salisbury in the eleventh century and is known as the *Sarum rite,* after the Latin word for Salisbury.

This fourteenth-century missal follows the rite used in York, which was popular until the Reformation in England. The illuminations are fairly simple, and, although they include the use of gold leaf, they are not of a particularly high quality, indicating that the original parish which owned this missal may not have been very wealthy. There are documents pasted into the front of the missal recording various property covenants between the priests of Tatham and local parishioners, which would strongly suggest that this book originated in the parish church of St James the Less at Tatham, in the Lune valley, north-east of Lancaster.

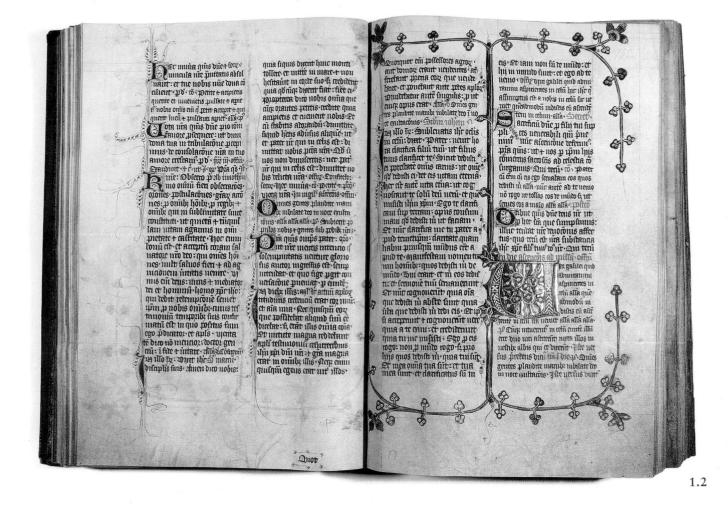

1.2

1.3

ALABASTER PANEL OF THE ADORATION OF THE MAGI
Alabaster, with traces of paint and gilding, 450 x 35 x 50mm
English, fifteenth century

This small panel once formed part of a larger altarpiece. This would have consisted of perhaps a dozen similar panels illustrating scenes from the life and Passion of Christ, flanked with saints. Traces of pigment and gilding are visible in places, giving the modern viewer a hint of the gorgeous, gaudy colours that would once have adorned the panel.

The scene shows Mary reclining with the infant Christ on her lap, His hand raised in blessing as He receives the gifts of gold, frankincense and myrrh from the Magi or three wise men. Below, the ox and ass eat hay calmly from a manger and St Joseph turns his head away from the scene, to remind the onlooker that although he was the protector of the infant Christ, he was not His father.

Like many pre-Reformation Catholic artefacts, this has an uncertain early history. It was found in the manor of Stonyhurst in 1794 when the building was given to the suppressed English Jesuits by the Weld family as a new home for the English Academy at Liège, the successor of St Omers College that the Jesuits had founded on the continent in 1593.

Stonyhurst was originally the home of the Shireburn family, many of whose sons had attended St Omers. They were a well-known Catholic family, of considerable wealth and influence in the north of England, and they enjoyed some immunity from the persecution that many of their fellow Catholics further south suffered.

An inventory of household goods at Stonyhurst in 1713 mentions this alabaster panel along with fourteen others, and records that they were located in the family chapel. This chapel dates from the 1590s, and, as the alabasters are at least a century older, it is likely that they were brought to Stonyhurst from elsewhere. There was a fifteenth-century Shireburn Chantry Chapel at nearby Mitton, which was dismantled on orders from Henry VIII during the Reformation. This is the most likely original source of these alabasters, and would explain why the original large altarpiece had been broken down into its component parts.

Alabaster is crystalline form of gypsum, and its milky translucent lustre made it highly prized for carving. It is soft and easily damaged by water, so it was never used outdoors. Nottingham and its surrounding area was famed for alabaster and was the centre of a huge industry in the fourteenth and fifteenth centuries, distributing carved panels and altarpieces all over Europe. No complete English example survived the iconoclasm of

1.3

the Reformation, but exported examples can still be seen on the continent, particularly in Germany, the Baltic and Scandinavia.

1.4
BOOK OF HOURS
Vellum, ink, pigments and gold leaf, 190 x 290mm
Paris, *circa* 1430

Many books of hours are known by the name of the person who originally commissioned them, or who owned them in later years. This beautiful French manuscript bears no name to identify its first, or, indeed, any subsequent, owner. It does, however, have a portrait of the woman who paid for it, and who ordered it to be laid out with such lavish and costly illuminations and gold leaf decoration.

She appears towards the back of the book and is shown kneeling, with her new prayer book, in front of the Virgin and Child. She is wearing a widow's hood, and simple, though rich, clothes. Was she perhaps recently bereaved and did she commission this book as a solace for her grief? What is certain is that she was left a substantial inheritance as the illuminations contained in the vellum pages are the work of a highly skilled and doubtless very well paid artist, and the decorations contain a liberal amount of 23-carat gold leaf.

The most expensive component in the book was not, however, the gold but the intense blue paint used for Mary's robes. It is ultramarine, a highly prized pigment which was made from pure Afghan lapis lazuli.

Ounce for ounce, it cost more than solid gold, and its use was always negotiated separately when a new book of hours was being commissioned. Such was its expense and prestige that it was invariably reserved for illustrations of members of the Holy Family.

Pious lay men and women bought books of hours so that they could join in the universal prayer of the Church, without having to cloister themselves in monasteries or convents. The great monastic orders of the Middle Ages arranged their day around sets of recited prayers, psalms and readings, from matins in the early hours of the morning and repeated throughout the day until darkness fell and vespers was sung.

A book of hours consisted of eight simplified groups of prayers and readings, designed to fit in with daily life outside the monastery walls, commencing at dawn, proceeding at regular intervals throughout the day and ending at bedtime. Books of hours were immensely popular in continental Europe and also in pre-Reformation England, where they were usually known as *primers*.

1.4

1.5

THE ST DUNSTAN CHASUBLE

1200 x 660mm

Mid-fifteenth century origins, reworked *circa* 1600

Loaned by the British Province of the Society of Jesus

A chasuble is the outer robe worn by a priest celebrating Mass. It evolved from a circular garment worn in ancient Greece, and was adopted by the early Church as a vestment some time in the fourth century. This chasuble, however, began life in a different form. It was originally a cope, a formal cloak worn by priests on ceremonial occasions, and the embroideries, or *orphreys* as they are known, would have made a decorative border for the front edges of the cope. The orphreys date from the mid-fifteenth century and most of them tell stories from the lives of saints and bishops associated with Canterbury. It is highly likely, therefore, that this cope was first made for use at Canterbury Cathedral.

The front orphreys depict the martyrdom of St Thomas Becket, who was murdered in Canterbury Cathedral in 1170, supposedly on the orders of Henry II, for upholding papal authority over that of the king. The back of the chasuble, which would have been the side seen by the congregation (as priests said Mass with their backs to the people until the mid-1960s) shows, on the left side, St Dunstan sitting in his workshop making gold and silver sacred vessels. He is tempted by the Devil, but, rather than succumb, the saint heats his tongs until they are red-hot and

pinches the Devil's nose. Below is St Blaise, who was put to death in the year 316 by having his flesh torn by iron combs. His relics were venerated at Canterbury Cathedral in the Middle Ages. The last figure on the left is the Archbishop of Canterbury, St Elphege, who was martyred by the Danes in 1012. The scenes on the right depict St Odo (*d.* 958), Archbishop of Canterbury, overcoming the disbelief of two clerics in the Real Presence of Christ, by causing blood to pour from the broken Host. The middle embroidery shows St Thomas Becket's relics healing a leprous boy in front of Stephen II. The final scene on the right is another miracle associated with the saint: a dead child was restored to life when placed on the spot where St Thomas had administered confirmation to the poor on his way to London.

The cope was probably hidden during the dissolution of the monasteries in the mid-1530s and during the ensuing Reformation, when Catholic artefacts were destroyed in large numbers. At some point it was smuggled out of England and sent to the college of the English Jesuits at St Omers. There the precious embroideries were cut away from the elderly and fraying fabric of the cope and were made into their present form as a chasuble.

1.5

1.6
THE LUCCA CHASUBLE
1210 x 630mm
English, *circa* 1450-1500

This gold chasuble and its embroideries were ordered and paid for by the wealthy Ludovico Bonvisi whose name is recorded on the back. The Bonvisi family were wealthy and influential merchant bankers from Lucca in Italy, who counted Henry VII, Henry VIII and Cardinal Wolsey among their clients. Antonio Bonvisi, possibly Ludovico's son, was born in England between 1470 and 1475 and was one of the closest friends of St Thomas More (1478-1535).

These beautiful English embroideries date from the second half of the fifteenth century, and the images chosen by Ludovico Bonvisi are of saints and scenes familiar to him in Lucca.

The back of the vestment shows the Annunciation, when the angel Gabriel foretold the birth of Christ to Mary, overlooked by God the Father holding the Dove of the Holy Spirit. This is an unusual choice for the back of a chasuble, which almost invariably shows the Crucifixion.

Beneath the feet of Mary and Gabriel is the trademark of the Bonvisi banking business and a request in Latin for prayers for Ludovico.

Below is one of the images most dear to the hearts of all natives of Lucca – the *Volto Santo*, or Holy Face of Christ. According to

tradition, Nicodemus, one of the witnesses of the Resurrection, with the aid of angels, carved the real likeness of Christ in the form of a crucifix. This crucifix reached Lucca in the eighth century, arriving in a boat guided by angels, and became the most prestigious and precious possession in the city's cathedral. The English embroiderer has declined to call it the *Volto Santo*, the name by which most Italians would have known it, but has sewn the words *The Rode of Lucca* beneath the crucifix. The word *rode*, or *rood*, was a Saxon name for a crucifix.

The bottom embroidery shows a female saint much beloved in Lucca, St Zita, here renamed in English fashion as St Sitha. Zita was a holy servant maid of Lucca, who spent much time instructing children in their catechism. She is shown here with her rosary, Bible and the keys of her mistress's household, indicating the great trust placed in her by her employers. According to St Thomas More, St Zita was a popular saint in England as well as in Lucca, and was much invoked as a reliable finder of lost keys.

During the Reformation, vestments such as these were outlawed, and most were destroyed. This one was hidden in a secret Jesuit mission house in England in the

1.6

seventeenth century and rediscovered in the early nineteenth century, when it was transferred to Stonyhurst. The original cloth of gold background had deteriorated beyond repair and in 1827 was replaced by the present silk cloth of gold.

29

1.7
THE LEAGRAM CHASUBLE
1290 x 600mm
Circa 1450

This blue and gold silk damask velvet chasuble is named after Leagram Hall, a medieval house near Chipping, in the Forest of Bowland in north Lancashire, largely rebuilt in the eighteenth century. There was a Catholic chapel at Leagram from its earliest days, and it is probable that the Hoghton family who lived there in the fifteenth century bought this vestment for use in their domestic chapel. The main branch of the family lived at nearby Hoghton Tower, which in Elizabethan times sheltered Edmund Campion and is reputed to have links with the young William Shakespeare.

The Hoghtons were a wealthy family, well able to afford the very expensive Genoese silk velvet fabric for this vestment. The embroidered orphreys are of the type known as *opus anglicanum,* or English work, which was famous and much sought after throughout Europe. The embroideries are particularly fine, with much gold thread work, and among the usual figures of saints and prophets is a charming scene of St Anne teaching the young Virgin Mary to read. The shape of the vestment would suggest that it has not been altered much, if at all, since it was first made.

Leagram Hall chapel continued to serve the Catholics of the parish of Chipping quietly throughout the Reformation and until 1828 when changes to the law forbidding Catholic worship in England allowed the building of a public parish church. The chasuble was kept at Leagram until 1953 when the Weld family, who had inherited the house in the eighteenth century from the Shireburns of Stonyhurst, passed it to Father Martin D'Arcy SJ (1888-1976), and he in turn presented it to Stonyhurst College.

1.7

Reformation

DEBORAH YOUNGS

When Henry VIII succeeded to the throne in 1509, England was a Catholic country which looked to the pope as its spiritual head. Ten years later, when the first stirrings of Protestantism were felt across continental Europe, England remained loyal both to the pope and to the idea of a united Christendom. Indeed, in 1521, the conservative Henry denounced the teachings of the reformer Martin Luther and was rewarded with the title *Defender of the Faith,* still borne by British monarchs to this day.

Moving forward another ten years, however, a very different picture emerges. Henry was now in opposition to Pope Clement VII who had refused to grant the king's wish to divorce his first wife, Katherine of Aragon, and wed his mistress, Anne Boleyn. The dispute would trigger a chain of events that revolutionised the religious landscape of England. Through a series of parliamentary acts, England "broke" with Rome and the king became the supreme head of the Church in England. From this position, Henry oversaw a decade of reforms. Between 1535 and 1540, the monasteries of England and Wales were completely dissolved. In 1536 pilgrimages were abolished and in 1538 royal injunctions were issued against the burning of candles before images. By Henry's death in 1547, practices that had once been at the heart of medieval popular religion, such as the cult of saints, had been redefined as superstitious and idolatrous.

Why did the king's marital problem lead to a reformation in religious beliefs and practices? This is a question that has fascinated historians for many years. It was once thought that the transformations initiated by Henry's government were timely interventions to cleanse a corrupt and moribund Church which had lost its way by the end of the Middle Ages. However, the evidence available today suggests a very different scenario: that the people of England and Wales, on the very eve of the Reformation, were deeply satisfied with their traditional forms of faith. There appears no waning in the enthusiasm for traditional practices such as the cult of saints or attending Mass.

In Liverpool, in the 1540s, the priest of "St John's altar" was to provide early morning Masses so that the town's labourers could attend divine service before work. Money poured into parish churches and investment in new buildings was high. In south Lancashire alone, thirty-eight new chapels were founded between 1500 and 1548. Parishioners financed the replacement of windows, the painting of images and the purchase of vestments. In the 1520s, Eccles church in Salford, for instance, benefited from generous bequests by John Booth of Barton, esquire, and Robert Langley of Agecroft Hall. Alongside these important communal aspects, the medieval Church took advantage of rising literacy rates and promoted the production and use of spiritual works. Wealthier members of society, such as Elizabeth of York and Cardinal Thomas Wolsey, could afford to buy hand-made, illuminated personal prayer books, known as books of hours. For the wider population, the new technology of printing (introduced into England in 1476) facilitated the dissemination of cheaper versions. Over one hundred separate editions of primers (as books of hours were called in England) were printed between 1501 and 1535 in order to satisfy demand. By all accounts late medieval religion was strong, vibrant and catering for all levels of society.

There is, therefore, no evidence to indicate widespread hostility to the Church, no great desire to jump on the bandwagon of evangelical Protestantism. Yet it does not mean that the Church was beyond criticism. It had clearly faced challenges for centuries, including the English heretical movement known as Lollardy. Early sixteenth-century England contained a growing minority who had become disillusioned with medieval Catholicism. While many who wanted to stay within the Catholic Church generated criticisms, they were increasingly influenced by the more radical writings of the continental reformers. By the 1520s, certain devotional practices were attracting criticism: there was a desire to remove images from churches and a growing reluctance to finance chantries where the clergy sang Masses for the souls of the dead. There are hints that radical preachers were finding an audience and that heretical networks were developing in London and the university colleges of Oxford and Cambridge.

Until the late 1520s, however, these views, branded heretical, had little chance of succeeding in England. What changed was Henry's challenge to the papacy. In justifying the break with Rome, Henry and his supporters had used the rhetoric of evangelical reformers to their advantage. In particular, they drew on Lutheran ideas concerning papal jurisdiction and the place of the ruler. The pope – whom they now called the bishop of Rome – was depicted as a usurper of authority and associated with superstition and error: his name was to be removed from service books. This encouraged a diluted form of Lutheranism to creep into court and the appointment of reformers to episcopal positions.

In the 1530s iconoclasm became a feature of south-eastern England. It was reported in London that images were being thrown out of churches as worthless bits and pieces. Official support was extended to attacks made on pilgrimages, the worship of saints, and purgatory. The cult of Thomas Becket was condemned by royal proclamation, which denounced the erstwhile saint as a rebel (for his opposition to Henry II in 1170). His great shrine at Canterbury was smashed, and orders were given for images and pictures of Becket to be destroyed, for his feast day to be abolished, and for his name to be erased from all liturgical books. The 1530s also saw an increase in publications written in English (rather than in Latin), reflecting the reformers' emphasis on direct access to the word of God. William Tyndale's translation of the New Testament found a ready market, especially among university men. Luther's works (albeit anonymously) began circulating in English, and by the 1540s the writings of the continental reformers Zwingli and Bucer were also available in translation.

In these ways, reformist ideas gained a foothold in English society, but support was neither immediate nor widespread. It would be wrong to see England as a Protestant country under Henry VIII. The king took his role as head of the Church seriously and he would not tolerate radicals, denying many doctrines central to Protestantism, such as justification by faith alone. His curbs on freedom of expression meant that the path taken by the Reformation in England was complex, gradual and piecemeal. At the same time, the government had to take account of political threats from Catholic rulers abroad, and from resistance at home.

While reformist ideas had gained ground in south-eastern England, the north held on to its late medieval Catholic faith and showed reluctance to support Henrician reforms. In Lancashire, preaching against the pope caused discontent. Neighbouring Cheshire was similarly slow to embrace change. In 1541, the first bishop of Chester, John Bird, complained that his region was full of "popish idolatry" and that the idols and images removed from churches were being kept for "ignorant people to offer as before". More dramatic resistance came when the dissolution of the monasteries sparked rebellions in Lancashire, Lincolnshire, Cumberland, and Yorkshire – the so-called Pilgrimage of Grace. With no standing army in England, the government was dependent on local gentry to enforce the reforms. For the port of Liverpool, under the influence of the conservative families of Stanley and Molyneux, this meant that evangelical reform made slow progress throughout the sixteenth century.

Alongside those who vociferously supported or clearly resisted Henry's reformation, there were the silent majority who were neither entirely behind reform nor entirely against it. On the whole, people did collaborate with the government in the sense that they dismantled shrines and informed against those who were loyal to the pope. Most noblemen, justices of the peace, clergy, churchwardens and constables obeyed the instructions given to them, not wishing to defy the power of the king. But it is difficult to know what people thought when they professed their loyalty, or why they wished to collaborate.

They would certainly have known that disobedience had serious consequences. Henry's response to Thomas More's opposition to the Act of Supremacy was a clear case in point: More was arrested, imprisoned in the Tower of London, and executed in July 1535. At the same time, it was not a movement carried away by momentum, powered by violence and bloodshed. The slow, piecemeal process meant that people in England never had to subscribe to a fully formed Reformation agenda. The incremental implementation helped make changes more acceptable and there were noticeable continuities with older religious practices. Churches still provided meeting places, and the key rites of passage of baptism, marriage and burial remained largely the same. Even though purgatory came under suspicion and was then officially abolished, civic elites of towns continued to commemorate their dead benefactors. The focus was now on good citizenship rather than on the demands of their souls. Plays, processions and pageants regularly took place.

While many feasts associated with saints ceased to exist, other gatherings, such as those at Whitsun, occurred throughout the sixteenth century.

Nevertheless, these continuities took place in a considerably altered context. By the mid-sixteenth century, English people saw the relationship between Church and state very differently. They were now undertaking actions that they would never have dreamt of doing thirty or even twenty years before, such as plundering the monasteries and reading an English Bible. More changes were on the way. The destruction of Catholic practices took a step further under Henry's son, Edward VI: from 1547, iconoclasm was officially sanctioned and the foundation of Protestant England was laid with the Book of Common Prayer (1549). Upheaval occurred again under Edward's sister, Mary, when, between 1553 and 1558, she set about reversing Protestant reforms and re-establishing Catholicism. In such tumultuous times, it is impossible to describe the typical experience or beliefs of people living during the Tudor reformations. But one thing is clear: the medieval religious world had gone.

2.1

RELIC OF THE HOLY THORN

Thorn, pearls, enamel, crystal and silver gilt, 300 x 100 x 100mm

Loaned by the British Province of the Society of Jesus

Perhaps the most renowned of the many relics housed and venerated at Stonyhurst College is the Holy Thorn, often called *Mary, Queen of Scots' Thorn*. It has a venerable and extraordinary history.

According to ancient tradition, this thorn was part of the Crown of Thorns forced onto the head of Jesus Christ at His Passion and Crucifixion. The Crown, along with the Cross and other relics of the Crucifixion, were hidden in Jerusalem for three centuries, until their location was revealed in a dream to St Helena (*circa* 250-330).

St Helena was the mother of the Emperor Constantine. Her conversion to Christianity in the fourth century claimed the Roman Empire for the religion that it had persecuted so vigorously for so long. Through Constantine, the relics of the Passion passed into the hands of the Byzantine imperial family and many made their way to Constantinople.

The Fourth Crusade reached Constantinople in 1204. Its leader, Count Baldwin, decided that there were richer pickings to be had by sacking the city, rather than venturing on the decidedly riskier prospect of seizing Jerusalem back from the Moors. Baldwin crowned himself emperor and seized as many of the assets of the imperial family as he could lay his hands on, including the Crown of Thorns.

In 1238, distinctly short of money, he pawned it to a consortium of Venetian merchants and finally sold it for 10,000 *livres* in 1239 to Louis IX (1214-1270), king of France – the future St Louis. The king brought the Crown and other relics back to France and built the exquisite Sainte-Chapelle in Paris as a fitting setting to hold them. There they remained for five hundred years until the French Revolution. In 1794 the mob broke in to the chapel, looted it and dispersed or destroyed its relics. The Crown was lost and all that remains of it today – in Notre Dame cathedral in Paris – is the mat of twisted reeds on which it once sat.

No fewer than one hundred and thirty authenticated thorns from the Crown still survive, thanks to the French royal family's generous habit over the centuries of breaking off individual thorns to present as gifts to worthy recipients. In 1558, the young Mary, Queen of Scots, was given a double thorn from the Crown in honour of her marriage to the French dauphin, subsequently François II (1544–1560). She left France a widow in 1560, but kept the two thorns with her at Holyrood in Edinburgh until her stormy reign in Scotland ended in flight to England in 1568. There, she continued her intrigues, plotting to usurp the English throne from her Protestant cousin, Elizabeth I.

To further this aim, Mary presented her ardent advocate, Thomas Percy (1528-1572), seventh Earl of Northumberland, with the double thorn. He wore it constantly in a gold crucifix until his execution for his part in the ill-fated 1569 rising of the northern earls. On the eve of his death in 1572, Percy gave the thorns to his daughter, Elizabeth Woodruffe, or Woodroff, who subsequently became a staunch friend of the Jesuits in England. In 1594, she gave both thorns to the Jesuit, Father John Gerard (1564-1637), as a gift to the Society of Jesus. Her friend, Jane Wiseman, of Braddocks in Essex, arranged for the two thorns to be divided and each was encased in the elaborate enamelled gold reliquary, which can be seen here. The pearls twined round the thorn reputedly belonged to Mary, Queen of Scots. On the base of the reliquary is an inscription crediting Elizabeth Woodroff and Jane Wiseman for their contribution to the new housing for the thorn.

Both reliquaries remained in London until 1665, when, at the height of the Great Plague, special arrangements were made in case death should overtake the Jesuits guarding them and in case the thorns should fall thereafter into the wrong hands. Both reliquaries were sent over to Flanders – one to St Omers and the other to the nearby English Jesuit noviciate at Watten.

The Watten thorn passed into the hands of the Bishop of Ghent in 1773, when the Jesuit order was suppressed: it can still be venerated today in the Church of St Michael the Archangel in Ghent. The remaining thorn moved with the college from St Omers to Bruges in 1762 and was seized there by Austrian troops in 1773 when the Jesuits were suppressed. The Austrians looted the college, and a group of pupils were so outraged at the treatment of their school and their beloved masters that they broke open the chained cupboard in which the thorn was kept. Hugh Clifford, aged seventeen, took the thorn and set out home for England in the company of another pupil and of an ex-Jesuit scholastic still undergoing his training. The little group broke their journey at the English Charterhouse, home of the exiled English Carthusians, at Nieuwpoort, on the Flemish coast, where they told the prior about the treasure they were carrying. He threatened the boys with excommunication for sacrilege, took possession of the thorn and promptly returned it to the Austrian authorities in Bruges.

There it remained until 1781 when a former pupil of the English Jesuits at Bruges, Thomas Weld (1750-1810), was travelling in the Low Countries. In Bruges, he heard about the thorn and, remembering it from his schooldays, determined to recover it. He visited the Bruges notary in whose custody it lay, offered him five guineas for the reliquary, and took the thorn back to his

2.1

estate at Lulworth in Dorset. The thorn was venerated in his private chapel for twenty-two years until 1803, when he generously presented it to his old school, which had been relocated at Stonyhurst College in Lancashire.

The beautiful Elizabethan reliquary of gold, enamel and rock crystal housing the Thorn has symbols of the Passion depicted around the sides. The modern case now housing it was made by Louis Osman (1914-1996) in 1963.

41

2.2

CARDINAL WOLSEY'S BOOK OF HOURS – USE OF SARUM

Stonyhurst Ms 57
Vellum, ink, pigment and gold leaf, 120 x 160mm
Circa 1400-1420

This tiny illuminated manuscript has an interesting history. The illuminations are Flemish, and specifically are typical of those produced by artists working in Bruges at the beginning of the fifteenth century. The lavishly decorated margins around the text are English in style. It appears, therefore, that the book has two sources of production. It is possible that an English patron ordered the illustrations from the continent, and that they were then bound into an English manuscript in London. Alternatively, the book could have been produced in Bruges for an English market, using English artists working abroad. The prayers and Mass settings used in the book are those of Sarum, or Salisbury: from this, it can be deduced that the book was originally intended for an English owner.

The book trade at this period was an international concern. Books were produced all over Europe for different markets, and skilled artists and scribes could find work in any major European city. Most manuscript workshops operated on a production line principle, producing the text in-house, farming out the illustrations to contracted artists and then sending the whole manuscript out to be collated and bound by a stationer.

The more lavish and expensive books were bespoke – made to the order of a wealthy patron, who gave specific instructions as to the choice of illuminations, quantity of gold leaf, and even which prayers and Masses were to be included. There was also a healthy trade in second-hand books of hours: such prestigious and expensive books often served generations of owners, were handed down in wills, or were bought and sold in used book shops. To own a book of hours was a sign of wealth, prestige and success over and above the book's primary purpose as a mark of personal piety and devotion.

There is an inscription on the flyleaf of this book stating that it was a gift from Cardinal Lorenzo Campeggio (1471/2–1539) to his brother cardinal in England, Thomas Wolsey (1470/71–1530).

Campeggio came to England in September 1528 as the representative of Pope Clement VII. His visit was ostensibly to hear the case of Henry VIII who had petitioned the pope for an annulment of his marriage to Katherine of Aragon, his brother's widow, whom he wished to put aside so as to marry again. In reality, Campeggio's brief from the pope was to delay the matter and to play for time, as the pope had no wish to offend either Henry or Katherine's powerful nephew, the Holy

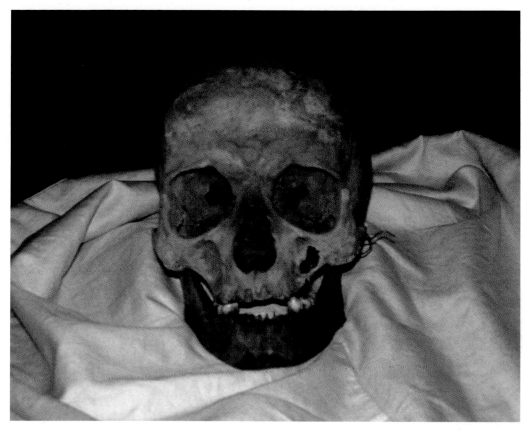

2.3

and broken, several parts of his body wrapt in divers Cere-cloths were taken away by rude and barbarous people. At length the head only remaining 'twas beg'd out of a pious mind purposely to save it of Dr Sheldon Archb[ishop] of Canterbury by Ralph Sheldon of Beoly in Worcestershire. Who esteeming it as a choice relique provided a leaden box to receive it and with great devotion kept it to his dying day An[no] 1684.

The skull remained in Sheldon possession down to the nineteenth century when several members of the Sheldon family became Jesuits and went to live at Stonyhurst. Though it is not known exactly how and when the skull arrived there, this family link presumably accounts for the fact that it came to be at Stonyhurst.

45

2.4

BOOK OF HOURS – USE OF SARUM
Stonyhurst Ms 35
Vellum, ink, pigment and gold leaf, 180 x 280mm
Circa **1430-1450**

From the dissolution of the monasteries under Henry VIII, through the purges of Edward VI, to the visitations of Elizabeth I, government commissioners rooted out almost all remnants of Catholic liturgical textiles or plate, devotional books or architectural features in parish churches throughout England. Despite this, there remain a small but significant number of pre-Reformation artefacts to bear witness to the rich artistic heritage of medieval England which is now largely lost.

This small book of hours demonstrates on its pages the effects of the Reformation on traditional religious practices. Henry VIII ordered that all mention of any pope and St Thomas Becket be struck from all prayer books, missals and manuals throughout the country. Henry had replaced the pope as head of the Church in England and so wished to remove his rival's name. Furthermore, he particularly wished to censor the name of Becket – a saint who had been martyred defending the authority of the pope over the English monarchy. In this book all references to either figure have been struck through with a red pen.

Henry VIII's son, Edward VI, although only sixteen when he became king, strongly believed that his father's reforms had not gone far enough. He ordered that all idolatrous images of saints, the Trinity, God, Jesus or Mary be removed from artworks, painted decoration, sculpture and devotional books. In this book of hours, the holy figures have literally been defaced. The text, however, of holy psalms, Gospel readings and traditional hymns have been left untouched.

During the reign of Edward's half-sister, Elizabeth I, from 1558 to 1603, the mere possession of such Catholic books was enough to earn the owner a hefty fine or imprisonment. Many books of this kind were destroyed: others, like this one, were smuggled abroad to continental Europe for safe keeping.

2.4

2.5

THE BOOK OF HOURS OF ELIZABETH PLANTAGENET (1466-1503)

Stonyhurst Ms 37
Vellum, ink, pigment and gold paint, 180mm x 290mm
Circa 1480

This simply bound velvet-covered book was the property of Princess Elizabeth Plantagenet, daughter of Edward IV, and better known to history as Elizabeth of York, later queen of Henry VII (1457-1509).

Elizabeth had a sheltered early childhood, suitable to a king's only daughter. She was blessed in her father's choice of tutor, John Morton (1420-1500). Bishop Morton was a learned man, with the gift of inspiring respect and affection in those he worked with. He formed a close bond with his young tutee and with her brothers, who also came under his charge. There is no doubt that Bishop Morton would have done his best to comfort the young princess when her brothers mysteriously vanished in the Tower of London in 1483, reputedly murdered by her uncle, Richard, who then laid claim to her recently dead father's throne as Richard III.

Elizabeth played little part in the civil war that followed, but she was persuaded by Bishop Morton to marry the victorious Henry Tudor, thus ensuring that the two warring dynasties of York and Lancaster would unite, and forge peace in England. By all accounts theirs was a warm and affectionate marriage, producing two sons and two daughters who lived to adulthood. Elizabeth was a pious and devout Catholic, regular in her observance of prayers and attendance at Mass. The queen's last pregnancy proved fatal. Her baby, Katherine, was born prematurely at the Tower of London on 2 February 1503, and Elizabeth died nine days later, on 11 February, her thirty-seventh birthday.

This book was given to her before her marriage, and so she signed it with her maiden name, *Elizabeth Plantagenet*. Some years later, after her coronation, she returned to the book and added her new title, *the quene*. It contains the usual prayers, Gospel readings, Masses for the dead and psalms normally to be found in a book of hours. The illuminations are beautiful, if simple, and are decorated not with solid gold leaf, as found in the more expensive books, but with gold paint made with gold dust, producing a sugary, sparkling effect.

2.5

2.6
HENRY VII CHASUBLE
1150 x 690mm
***Circa* 1490**
Loaned by the British Province of the Society of Jesus

This chasuble was once a cope, or ceremonial cloak, and was part of a set of twenty-nine, ordered and paid for by Henry VII in the late 1480s or 1490s. The design is worked in crimson silk velvet on cloth of gold tissue woven in Florence. It combines the red rose of Lancaster, and the portcullis badge of the Beaufort family, of which Henry's mother was a member. The copes were intended for use in Westminster Abbey at the great feasts of the pre-Reformation Catholic Church. Precious enough to be named specifically in Henry's will, they were bequeathed to

> God and St Peter, and to the Abbot, Prior and Convent of our monastery at Westminster, that now, and hereafter shall be, for a perpetual memory, there to remain while the world shall endure.

Henry VII's son, Henry VIII, took all twenty-nine copes with him to France to enhance his sumptuous and gaudy display at the Field of the Cloth of Gold. At this three-week meeting, held near Calais (7-24 June 1520), Henry VIII and the young French king, François I, tried to out-dazzle each other with wealth and glitter. The meeting nearly bankrupted the treasuries of France and England and proved useless politically.

The pious intentions of Henry VII were short-lived. The world he knew was soon to be cast away by his son during the Reformation, and, in the chaos of the dissolution of the monasteries that followed Henry VIII's break with Rome, many of the copes vanished and were presumed destroyed. By 1608 there were only eleven left in existence in England: Oliver Cromwell's Puritans burned these in 1643, during the English civil war.

Somehow, between the end of Henry VIII's reign and the beginning of the seventeenth century, two copes were smuggled away from the main body of vestments. By 1609 they had made their way secretly across the Channel to the English Jesuit college at St Omers. There they were preserved as a precious memento of England's Catholic heritage. As one of the copes had been damaged, it was cut down for use as this chasuble. In 1827 the orphreys, or embroideries, were described as being very worn, and they were carefully restored by the Warrington-born sacristan at Stonyhurst College, Brother James Houghton (1796-1876), who had trained as a military tailor before becoming a Jesuit in 1816.

The cope and chasuble were last worn in

2.6

the 1990s during a visit of Queen Elizabeth II, when, as an ecumenical gesture, they were lent by Stonyhurst College to the Anglican Cathedral in Blackburn.

2.7
PRECES VARIAE
Stonyhurst Ms 45
Vellum, ink, pigment and gold paint, 160mm x 220mm
***Circa* 1500**

The Latin title of this exquisite manuscript means *Various Prayers,* and it was produced originally for the French royal family for their use at Mass in the Sainte-Chapelle in Paris. This beautiful thirteenth-century chapel, with its unparalleled stained glass windows, was created to house the relics of the Passion collected by Louis IX (1214-1270), king of France – the future St Louis.

Such was the fame of the collection, which included the Crown of Thorns and a large piece of the True Cross, that a special feast day was granted to the French royal family to celebrate the relics of the Passion. The prayers and setting for this Mass are included in this small prayer book, along with many beautiful illuminations showing the relics surrounded by brilliantly coloured angels.

The book is open at the folio showing the collection of relics in the sacristy in the Sainte-Chapelle. The ciborium on the right contains the Crown of Thorns, a piece of which can be seen in this same case, and, beneath it, a gold reliquary holding the supposed head of John the Baptist.

Most of this famous collection of relics was lost during the French revolution.

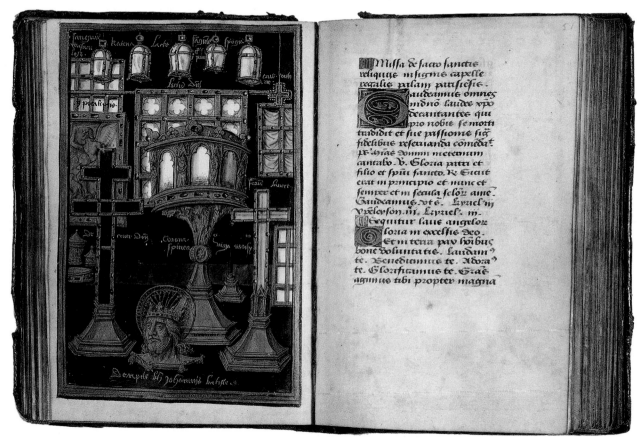

Missa de sacro sanctis
reliquis insignis capelle
regalis pilam paristensie.
Gaudeamus omnes
in dño laudes xpo
decantantes qui
pro nobis se morti
tradidit et sue passionis sig
fidelibus reseruanda comeda.
Et xpiae dominu meternum
cantabo. v. Gloria patri et
filio et spiritu sancto. Sicut
erat in principio et nunc et
semper et in secula selon ame.
Gaudeamus. vt e. Kyriel in
Kyeleyson. in. Kyriel. in.
Sequitur laus angeloz
Gloria in excelsis deo.
Et in terra pax homibus
bone voluntatis. laudam
te. Benedicimus te. Adora
te. Glorificamus te. Gratias
agimus tibi propter magna

2.7

2.8

HAT OF ST THOMAS MORE (1478-1535)

Felted wool and silk, 200 x 400 x 400mm (case)
Circa *1510-1520*
Loaned by the British Province of the Society of Jesus

Thomas More was, at the height of his career, one of the most successful and respected statesmen at the court of Henry VIII. He was renowned for his wisdom, his wit and his scrupulous honesty. The familiar image we have of him derives from his portrait by Hans Holbein, showing a wealthy courtier in fur and silks with a heavy gold chain, indicating his status as Chancellor of England.

As a young man, however, he struggled to earn a living as a lawyer and member of parliament, often finding it hard to make ends meet. More's story is well known. He fell from favour and office when he was unable to support Henry VIII in the matter of the king's divorce from his first wife, Katherine of Aragon. Initially, Henry agreed to sideline his old friend, and not to include him in the process, as he respected More's integrity and had no wish to cause him harm. But it was inconceivable that such an eminent and influential man should be left out of the controversy: Henry desperately needed his public support. More's conscience could not permit him to agree with the king's divorce, or to sign the oath of supremacy which repudiated the pope's authority and made Henry head of the church in England. To widespread shock and disapproval, Henry

VIII signed his old friend's death warrant and Thomas More was beheaded on Tower Green on 6 July 1535.

This simple brown hat dates from the early period of his life. It found its way to Stonyhurst by a very circuitous route. Thomas More had a wide circle of acquaintances amongst the learned men of Europe. Especially in his earlier years, he frequently travelled abroad to discuss the issues of the day with such men as the famous scholar, Erasmus of Rotterdam. Was the hat perhaps left behind on a visit to friends in the Netherlands? It is not known how it came about, but, by the early seventeenth century, this hat was in the hands of Godfrey Gillekens, Chancellor of the Supreme Court of Guelderland in the Low Countries. He clearly revered More's memory as he wore the hat in court every year on the anniversary of the saint's death. In 1654 Gillekens gave the hat to the Jesuit college at Roermond, whence it passed to the English Jesuit college in Bruges. In 1773, when the pope suppressed the Jesuit order, the hat passed into the possession of the parish priest of St Michael's Church in Brussels. In 1809 he gave it to a pious lady, Mademoiselle Thérèse Gaillard. When she was dying, she decided that the hat should be

2.8

restored to English hands, and, in 1835, it was brought to the Jesuits at Stonyhurst where it has remained ever since.

Thomas More was canonised in 1930. In 2000, Pope John Paul II declared him the patron saint of politicians and statesmen.

2.9

THE ARAGON CHASUBLE
1140 x 670mm
1534-1536?

According to tradition, this chasuble, and its accompanying set of dalmatics, were made by Queen Katherine of Aragon (1485-1536) and her ladies during her imprisonment at Kimbolton in Huntingdonshire between May 1534 and her death there on 7 January 1536.

Katherine had refused to accept that her marriage to Henry VIII was invalid. After many years of legal and political wrangling, Henry grew tired of waiting for the pope to agree with him and grant him an annulment from Katherine. In 1534, he broke with the Catholic Church, set himself up as supreme head of the Church in England and divorced Katherine. As she still refused to accept the situation, Henry put Katherine under house arrest in the manor of Kimbolton.

It is thought that the vestments were subsequently moved to Canterbury Cathedral. James II, the last Catholic king of England, presented them to the English Jesuits of St Omers College in the late 1680s.

The embroideries and the red silk velvet of the chasuble were much decayed by 1839, and were then heavily restored by Brother James Houghton, the sacristan at Stonyhurst College. It is difficult to tell how much of the original embroidery remains, although Brother Houghton recorded that the leaves and grapes were cut from the original fabric, repaired and then sewn on to the new silk velvet backing. The design shows grapes, which symbolise the blood of Christ, and the Dove of the Holy Spirit.

Over the centuries, these vestments were traditionally worn at the successive colleges of the English Jesuits at St Omers, Bruges, Liège and Stonyhurst on two special days each year – Whit Sunday, the feast of Pentecost, the birthday of the Church and the feast of the Holy Spirit, and on 1 December, the feast-day of the Jesuit martyrs, Edmund Campion, Alexander Briant and Ralph Sherwin, all executed on that day in 1581 at Tyburn in London.

2.9

2.10
THE BOOK OF HOURS OF MARY, QUEEN OF SCOTS (1542-1587)
Silk damask velvet, silk plush, enamelled gilt, silver gilt, 160 x 90mm
1558
Loaned by the British Province of the Society of Jesus

By venerable tradition, this book is believed to have been the property of Mary, Queen of Scots. Although there is little contemporary documentary evidence to support this, the attribution is of very long standing.

The book began its existence as the property of another famous queen of the same name. Mary Tudor (1516-1558), daughter of Henry VIII and Katherine of Aragon, became queen of England in 1553. Mary was a Catholic who had clung to her faith through the religious upheavals of the reigns of her father and brother, at great personal cost. When she ascended the throne, it was her intention to restore England to the Roman Catholicism of her early childhood.

The book consists of a traditional collection of prayers, psalms, Gospel readings and hymns such as had been used in Europe for centuries. It differs from the illuminated manuscripts in this exhibition in that it was printed and has no pictorial images. The plainness of the interior, however, is more than compensated for by the lavish decoration on the binding. The rich red silk damask is skilfully woven to be patterned on the upper side of the fabric and to have a rich brown silk pile on the underside, resembling fur. The velvet continues beyond the bottom edge of the book in a style known as *chemise* binding, allowing the silk 'fur' on the underside of the fabric to be seen and admired.

On the front of the book are silver gilt letters spelling out the queen's name in Latin, *Maria*. Flanking the letter *R*, are a tiny gold Tudor rose and a gold pomegranate, the badge of Mary's mother, Katherine of Aragon. On the back is the word *Regina*, meaning *Queen*, and Mary's royal coat of arms in enamel on gold. The book was ordered from a prestigious firm of publishers and bookbinders in Lyon.

The publication date of 1558 is significant. It was the year of Mary's death, and we can speculate that the book did not reach the English queen. Instead the only other person who could possibly have used it acquired it – another Catholic Queen Mary with Tudor blood and a claim to the royal arms of England – Mary, Queen of Scots, who in 1558 was married to the dauphin, the eldest son of the king of France.

According to tradition, Mary used the book in France and later in her native Scotland. It then travelled with her into exile and imprisonment in England. She is reputed to have read her last prayers from the book on the scaffold at Fotheringay, before her

2.10

execution in 1587 on the orders of her cousin, Elizabeth I, Mary Tudor's half-sister.

The book was smuggled away by Mary's companions and hidden for seventy years before it arrived at the college of the English Jesuits in Liège in 1650. It made its way to Lancashire in 1794 when the suppressed Jesuits of Liège were forced to flee the French revolutionary army advancing on the city and found themselves a new home at Stonyhurst.

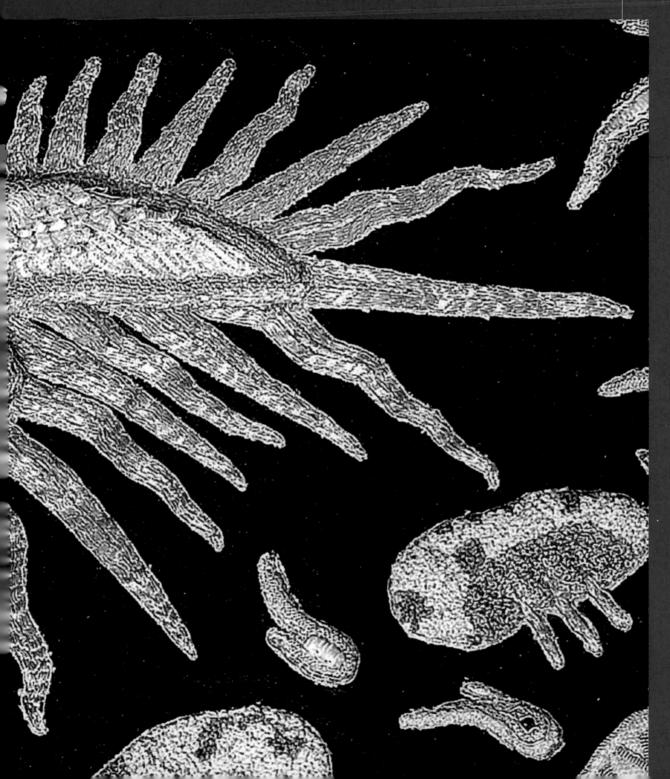

Catholic Recusancy in Lancashire in the Sixteenth and Seventeenth Centuries

J. A. HILTON

The Elizabethan settlement of 1559 brought to an end thirty years of religious change initiated by the crown. During this period, England had lurched from Catholicism to Protestantism, back to Catholicism, and finally back to Protestantism. The settlement consisted of two acts of parliament: the Act of Supremacy, which replaced the authority of the papacy in the English Church with that of the crown; and the Act of Uniformity, which replaced the Latin, Catholic service books with the English, Protestant Book of Common Prayer. The clergy and the holders of public office were required to take an oath accepting the royal supremacy on pain of deprivation, and everyone was required to attend the new Sunday services of the Church of England on pain of a fine for each absence of one shilling (five new pence, but a good day's wage in 1559). Such absence from church was the crime of *recusancy* (from the Latin verb, *recusare – to refuse*) and the guilty were called recusants.[1]

Among the few members of the clergy who refused to accept the Elizabeth settlement was Laurence Vaux (1519-1585), the warden of Manchester collegiate church (now the Anglican cathedral), then the most important church in Lancashire. His leadership was decisive in the formation of a recusant Catholic community in the county. Rather than take the oath of supremacy, Vaux went to join other English Catholic exiles in Louvain in the Spanish Netherlands (now Belgium). In 1566, he went to Rome where the pope asked him to return to England to make known the papal ruling that English Catholics could not in conscience attend the services of the Protestant Church of England.[2] Vaux made his way back to Lancashire where he circulated a letter proclaiming the papal ruling amongst the Catholic gentry:

> ... all such as offer children to the baptism now used or be present at the communion or service now used in churches in England, as well the laity as the clergy, do not walk in the state of salvation; ... there is no exception nor dispensation can be had for any of the laity if they will stand in the state of salvation.[3]

Vaux presented Catholics with a stark choice between conformity and Catholicism. A few responded positively to Vaux's appeal, enough to form the nucleus of the largest recusant community in England.

Meanwhile, another Lancastrian, William Allen (1532-1594), founded the English seminary at Douay (Douai, also then in the Spanish Netherlands), ensuring a supply of English priests to supplement the recusant clergy ordained under Henry VIII or Mary. Subsequently, seminaries were also founded at Rome (1579), Valladolid (1589), Seville (1592), and Lisbon (1628). Boys educated at home or in grammar schools, such as that at Blackburn, still under Catholic influence, or at clandestine Catholic schools, like that at Ormskirk, made their way to the continental seminaries to complete their education. They were then ordained as priests. Sixty out of 815 English seminary priests ordained during the reign of Elizabeth came from Lancashire.[4] Their aim, according to William Allen, was "to train Catholics to be plainly and openly Catholics".[5] These seminary or secular priests were eventually joined by the Jesuits, members of a new religious order, the Society of Jesus, founded in 1540 with a special vow of obedience to the pope and a commitment to missionary activity.[6]

As a result, a Catholic recusant community emerged in Lancashire, and, despite persecution, increased in numbers. In 1578 there were 304 convicted recusants in Lancashire and 29 non-communicants, that is, Catholics who attended the Anglican services but who refused communion.[7] By 1601 the number of recusants had more than doubled to 754, and the number of non-communicants had increased over ten-fold to 349. Nevertheless, they remained only a small minority, less than half a percent of an estimated population of one hundred thousand.[8] Catholic recusants were strongest in number in the south-west of the county. In 1596 there were only three in the deanery of Furness, 16 in Kendal, 25 in Lonsdale, and 16 in Manchester, but there were 45 in Leyland, 61 in Blackburn, 140 in Amounderness, and 465 in the deanery of Warrington.[9] Catholics were represented at almost every level of society from the gentry, through farmers, shopkeepers, craftsmen, and labourers, down to paupers and vagrants. They were, however, dominated by the gentry. In 1590, thirty per cent of the Lancashire gentry families were recusant, and, in 1596, twenty per cent of the Lancashire recusants were gentry. Moreover, not only did women outnumber male recusants, but also many of the conformist gentry had recusant wives and, therefore, recusant children.[10]

Faced with this resistance and alarmed both by Catholic plots on behalf of Mary, Queen of Scots, Elizabeth's rival for the English throne, and by Spanish aggression, the government responded with penal laws against the Catholics. It was forbidden to defend papal supremacy on pain of forfeiture of property; the fine for recusancy was increased to £20 a month; it was made treason to call the monarch a heretic, to introduce a papal bull, to convert or to be converted to Catholicism, and for a seminary priest or Jesuit to enter the country; and recusants were forbidden to travel further than five miles from their homes. Enforcement of these laws was patchy and erratic, depending on the willingness of local officials to apply them, and on the sensitivity of the central government to external threats. Indeed, the number of recusants in Lancashire continued to increase from 498 in 1598, to 754 in 1601, and to nearly 2,000 in 1603. The Gunpowder Plot of 1605 led to further anti-Catholic legislation: convicted recusants were compelled to receive the Anglican communion once a year on pain of a fine and eventual forfeiture of their possessions; a new oath of loyalty was imposed upon them; and they were barred from public office and the learned professions. If the penal laws did not exterminate Catholics, they at least restricted them to a small and persecuted minority.[11]

This minority, however, was at its strongest in Lancashire. As the new king, James I, wrote: "At our first entering to this Crown and Kingdom we were informed, and that too truly, that our county of Lancaster abounded more in popish recusants than any other country of England".[12] Catholics slipped back and forth between non-communicating conformity and recusancy, as the Jesuit, John Gerard (1564-1637), pointed out:

> When a large number of people are Catholics and nearly all have leanings towards Catholicism, it is easy to make many converts and to have large congregations at sermons. For instance, in Lancashire, I have seen myself more than two hundred present at Mass and sermon. People of this kind come into the Church without difficulty, but they fall away the moment persecution blows up. When the alarm is over they come back again.[13]

In 1601 there were 754 recusants and 349 non-communicants in Lancashire, and in 1604 the number of recusants had increased to 3,516 and the non-communicants to 521.[14]

The English Benedictines joined the seminary priests and Jesuits on the Lancashire mission. Anselm Beech (1568-1634), born in Manchester, was a seminary priest who joined a Benedictine monastery in Padua. He persuaded the papacy to allow English Benedictines to go on the English mission, which he did himself, seeking out the last surviving monk of Westminster Abbey in order to revive the English Benedictine Congregation.[15]

Increasing numbers of Lancastrian women, thirty-two between 1603 and 1642, entered the newly founded English convents on the continent, mainly the Augustinian Canonesses at Louvain and the Poor Clares at Gravelines. These religious houses were dependent on the generosity of Lancashire gentry, such as Thomas Worthington of Blainscough, the benefactor of the Augustinian Canonesses at Louvain. Members of the same family tended to follow one another into the same house. Thus there were four Clopton girls at Louvain and four Bradshaigh girls at Gravelines.[16]

As the conflict between Charles I and parliament grew worse, the Catholics were warned that their condition would "much alter ... either to the better or the worse, according as we shall express ourselves affectionate or cold" to the royalist cause.[17] As a result, the Catholic gentry flocked to join the royalist army in Lancashire in such numbers that it was known as "the Catholic army". The defeat of the king led to the confiscation of the property of active royalists, of whom the majority in Lancashire were Catholics.[18]

The restoration of the monarchy in 1660 in the person of a tolerant king, Charles II, led to some relaxation in the enforcement of the penal laws, despite a temporary persecution following the so-called and non-existent Popish Plot of 1678. During these years the Lancashire Catholic community continued to grow and became by far the largest of any county: in 1671 the recusant population of England was estimated at just over ten thousand and that of Lancashire at over five thousand. At the same time the Puritans abandoned the Church of England to form their own nonconformist churches, which were also persecuted.[19]

The accession of James II, the Catholic convert king, in 1685 brought toleration for Catholics and indeed political power. The king abandoned the application of the penal laws, permitted a number of Catholics to hold public office, and then in 1687 issued a declaration of indulgence suspending all the penal laws. Next, he handed over the administration of Lancashire to its Catholics. Lord Molyneux, a Catholic, was appointed lord lieutenant and members of the Catholic gentry became county magistrates. In Wigan, Thomas Gerard of Ince, also a Catholic, was appointed mayor and publicly attended Mass in the newly built Jesuit chapel there.

Meanwhile, a Catholic bishop or vicar apostolic, John Leyburn (1620-1702), was appointed for England and Wales, and toured the country administering confirmation. In 1688 a bishop for the north, including Lancashire, was appointed. The king's policies, however, united the Protestant majority against him, and he was overthrown in the Glorious Revolution of 1688. The penal laws were again enforced. For the next fifty years, the terms *Catholic* and *Jacobite* (a supporter of the exiled James II and his successors) became almost synonymous.[20] The attitude of the Lancashire Catholic community was summed up in the inscription erected at Aldcliffe, near Lancaster, by the spinster sisters of the Catholic royalist Thomas Dalton, who was killed in the Civil War: *CATHOLICAE VIRGINES NOS SUMUS: MUTARE VEL TEMPORE SPERNIMUS. ANNO DOMINI 1674* [We are Catholic virgins: we certainly scorn to change with the time. AD 1674].[21]

1 Christopher Haigh, *English Reformations: Religion, Politics, and Society under the Tudors* (Oxford, 1993), passim.

2 Robert Livesey, *Laurence Vaux: The Last Catholic Warden of the Manchester Collegiate Church 1519-1585* (Wigan, 2007), pp. 4-7.

3 T. G. Law (ed.), *A Catechisme or Christian Doctrine by Laurence Vaux* (Chetham Society, Manchester, new series, IV), pp. xxxii-xxxix.

4 Godfrey Anstruther, *The Seminary Priests* (4 vols., Great Wakering, 1968-77), I, pp. x-xii; P.W. Armitage, 'Catholicism and Educational Control in North-East Lancashire in the Reign of Elizabeth', *North West Catholic History* XIII (1986), pp. 1-9; A.C.F. Beales, *Education under Penalty* (London, 1961), pp. 74-83.

5 Philip Hughes, *The Reformation in England* (3 vols., London, 1963), pp. 282-302.

6 Henry Foley, *Records of the English Province of the Society of Jesus* (7 vols., London, 1877-83), V, pp. 1-262, 318-418.

7 Haigh, *Reformation and Resistance*, pp. 280, 289.

8 John K. Walton, *Lancashire: A Social History, 1558-1939* (Manchester, 1987), p. 47.

9 *Miscellanea* (Catholic Record Society, LIII, 1960), pp. 74-87, 101-107.

10 Walton, p. 46; Haigh, *Reformation and Resistance*, pp. 260-61, 281-85; John Bossy, *The English Catholic Community 1570-1850* (London, 1975), pp. 153-58; Marie B. Rowlands (ed.), *English Catholics of Parish and Town 1558-1578* (London, 1999), pp. 3-130; John Callow and Michael Mullett, 'The Shireburns of Stonyhurst: memory and survival in a Lancashire Catholic recusant family' in Richard Dutton, Alison Findlay and Richard Wilson (eds.), *Region, Religion and Patronage: Lancastrian Shakespeare* (Manchester, 2003), pp. 169-185.

11 Haigh, *Reformation and Resistance*, p. 330; Hughes, III, pp. 335-396; Godfrey Davies, *The Early Stuarts* (Oxford, 1959), pp. 204-11.

12 Haigh, *Reformation and Resistance*, p. 275.

13 C.P. Caraman (ed.), *The Hunted Priest: The Autobiography of John Gerard* (London, 1959), p. 50.

14 Haigh, *Reformation and Resistance*, pp. 277, 330.

15 Dom Henry Norbert Birt, *Obit Book of the English Benedictines 1600-1912* (Edinburgh, 1913), p. 16; David Lunn, *The English Benedictines 1540-1688* (London, 1980), pp. 25-26.

16 M.A. Tierney (ed.), *Dodd's Church History of England* (5 vols., London, 1839-49), IV, p. 107; Odo Blundell, *Old Catholic Lancashire* (3 vols., London, 1915-39), III, pp. 199-209.

17 Godfrey Anstruther, *Vaux of Harrowden* (London, 1953), p. 464.

18 B.G. Blackwood, *The Lancashire Gentry and the Great Rebellion* (Chetham Society, 3rd series, XXV, Manchester, 1978), passim; J.M. Gratton, 'The Earl of Derby's Catholic Army', *Transactions of the Historic Society of Lancashire and Cheshire*, CXXXVII (1988), p. 33; *Royalist Composition Papers* (Record Society of Lancashire and Cheshire, Manchester, XXIV, 1891, XXXVI, 1898, XCV, 1941, XCVI, 1942), passim.

19 *Miscellanea 6* (Catholic Record Society, London, VI, 1909), p. 77; B.G. Blackwood, 'Plebeian Catholics in Later Stuart Lancashire', *Northern History*, XXV (1989), p. 160.

20 John Miller, *Popery and Politics in England 1660-1688* (Cambridge, 1973), passim; G.A. Fallon, 'The Catholic Justices of Lancashire under James II', *North West Catholic History* [hereafter *NWCH*], VIII (1981), pp. 3-15; J.A. Hilton, 'Wigan Catholics and the Policies of James II', *NWCH*, I (3) (1969), pp. 97-110; J.A. Hilton, A.J. Mitchinson, Barbara Murray and Peggy Wells (eds.), *Bishop Leyburn's Confirmation Register of 1687* (Wigan, 1997), passim; Hilton, *Catholic Lancashire: From Reformation to Renewal 1559-1991* (Chichester, 1994), pp. 1-59.

21 *Victoria County History of Lancaster* (8 vols., London, 1906), VIII, p. 49.

3.1

PORTRAIT OF ST EDMUND CAMPION SJ (*circa* 1540-1581)
Pencil on paper, 480 x 400mm
Copied by Charles Weld, *circa* 1850, from a seventeenth-century portrait

Edmund Campion was one of the most famous Jesuits of his day. He was born around 1540 into a family of London booksellers and was brought up in the Anglican faith. From an early age he showed signs of a brilliant intellect and was brought to the attention of the young queen, Elizabeth I, while he was a student at the University of Oxford. He remained at Oxford as a fellow and planned a career in the Church of England. However, he began to have doubts about his faith and eventually travelled to the continent to become a Catholic priest, studying in Rome. His loss was keenly felt in England.

In 1580 he was sent back to England as a missionary priest. Catholics in England were confused about the new laws forbidding them to attend Mass, and needed guidance, support and encouragement, as well as the sacraments, access to which was becoming increasingly difficult and dangerous. Campion was a gifted speaker, and his sermons were famous: Catholics flocked to hear him, greatly endangering his safety. English government officials were very anxious to capture him, both to put an end to his work, and in the hope that they might persuade him to renounce his Catholicism. In 1581, Campion secretly published and distributed a book outlining the ten reasons on which his Church based its authority. Six weeks later he was betrayed and captured. Despite torture and public interrogation, Campion held fast to his faith. He was condemned to be hanged, drawn and quartered at Tyburn in London on 1 December 1581.

This pencil sketch is taken from a seventeenth-century painting of Edmund Campion, now lost, that once hung in Rome. Charles Weld, a former pupil of Stonyhurst College, copied it in the 1850s.

3.1

3.2

THE PEDLAR'S CHEST

Softwood, pony skin and printed paper, silk brocade, silk velvet, linen and various materials,
400 x 840 x 360mm
Circa 1600-1630

This seventeenth-century wooden chest covered with pony skin is of a type popular with travelling salesmen, or pedlars, who sold threads, sewing materials and small domestic implements from door to door. The chest was strapped onto the back of a packhorse, enabling access to distant rural households. It is possible that a Catholic priest working in secret in the Lancashire area used this chest. Priests were obliged to work under cover, often impersonating tradesmen who were freely able to travel from house to house without arousing suspicion.

The chest was found in the mid-nineteenth century, walled up in a compartment in a well-known Lancashire Catholic house, Samlesbury Hall, near Preston. Samlesbury was a centre for Catholic priests during the reigns of Elizabeth I and James I, and it is likely that the vestments found in the chest were in use by priests working in Lancashire during those years. There is evidence to link them to the Lancashire martyr, St Edmund Arrowsmith, who was hanged, drawn and quartered at Lancaster in 1628.

The contents include almost everything that a priest would have needed to say Mass: altar cloths, vestments, an altar stone, a chalice, and even a small rosary bracelet. The vestments are mostly pieced and patched from other garments, perhaps from women's worn-out dresses, which were turned into chasubles and stoles for the secret mission priests. On the top of the vestments there is a neatly folded pink silk bonnet dating from the early seventeenth century. This may have been included deliberately to conceal the incriminating vestments below. Alternatively, it could simply have been bundled into the chest by mistake at some point in its history.

3.2

3.3

PORTRAIT OF EDWARD OLDCORNE SJ (1561-1606)
Pencil on paper, 480mm x 400mm
Copied by Charles Weld, *circa* 1850, from a seventeenth-century portrait

Edward Oldcorne was born in York in 1561 to a Protestant father and a Catholic mother. He attended St Peter's School in that city, where three of his classmates were eventually to become part of the Gunpowder Plot – Guy Fawkes and the two brothers, John and Christopher Wright.

Edward intended originally to be a doctor, but changed his mind and went abroad to become a Jesuit priest, entering the Society of Jesus in 1588. He returned to England later that same year and was sent to Hindlip Hall in Worcestershire, a remote Catholic house, where he was to remain for the next seventeen years – one of the longest periods of ministry of any Jesuit serving in England.

During the furious hunt for those involved in the Gunpowder Plot after its discovery in 1605, three Jesuits fled from London and sought sanctuary at Hindlip. Father Henry Garnet, Brother Ralph Ashley and Brother Nicholas Owen were high on the government's wanted list, despite having had no involvement in the Plot. The authorities tracked them to Hindlip and the three of them, together with Edward Oldcorne, were forced to hide in specially prepared secret hiding holes. After four days, two of the men had to come out of hiding: the other two, one of whom was Father Oldcorne, held out for another four intolerable days before they gave themselves up. All of the Jesuits were tortured in the hope that they would give away others. Oldcorne was racked for five hours a day on five consecutive days, but was innocent of any involvement in the Plot. He was convicted of treason on the capital charge of being a priest and was hanged, drawn and quartered at Worcester on 7 April 1606. He was beatified, together with Ralph Ashley, in 1929, and Nicholas Owen was canonised in 1970.

This pencil sketch is taken from an original contemporary painting of Edward Oldcorne, now lost, that once hung in Rome. Charles Weld, a former pupil of Stonyhurst College, copied it in the 1850s.

3.3

3.4

RELIC OF BLESSED EDWARD OLDCORNE SJ (1561-1606)

Silver case, 70 x 70mm
Circa 1606

This silver locket contains the right eye of Edward Oldcorne. It was collected at the scene of his execution at Red Hill, near Worcester, in 1606 by a sympathetic Catholic. Father Oldcorne was hanged, drawn and quartered – a particularly vicious method of execution. The victim was half-hanged until he began to pass out, then was cut down and disembowelled while still alive, then castrated and finally his heart was removed. The body was then decapitated and cut into quarters and parboiled before being displayed at prominent sites around the city as a warning to future traitors.

The force of the axe-blow that cut off Father Oldcorne's head caused the eyeball to leave its socket, and an unknown sympathiser quickly picked it up as a precious relic of a martyr. The silver eye-shaped case dates from the same time, and the eyeball was sent to St Omers early in the seventeenth century. It was placed in the Sodality Chapel there, along with many other relics of English martyrs.

3.4

3.5

PORTRAIT OF ST EDMUND ARROWSMITH SJ (1585-1628)
Oil on canvas, 850 x 740mm
Nineteenth-century copy of a seventeenth-century portrait

Edmund Arrowsmith is one of the group of forty men and women martyred in England and Wales during the sixteenth and seventeenth centuries for practising their Catholic faith. They were canonised in 1970 and are usually known as the *Forty Martyrs*.

Edmund Arrowsmith was born at Haydock in Lancashire in 1585 to parents who were frequently imprisoned for their faith. On one occasion they were arrested in the middle of the night and dragged away to prison, leaving their four young children alone in the house, including Edmund, who was then only one year old. When he was twenty, Edmund travelled to France to study for the priesthood and became a Jesuit, returning to Lancashire eight years later to begin in secret his work as a missionary priest. He was based in various safe houses, but a Catholic who had a grudge against him betrayed him in 1628. He had time to hide his Mass vestments and chalice in the house before riding away, but he was captured when his horse refused to jump a stream at Brindle, near Preston. At Lancaster Castle, he was tried for high treason – the charge brought against all Catholic priests whose presence in England was outlawed. Found guilty, he was hanged, drawn and quartered at Lancaster on 28 August 1628.

3.5

3.6
THE ST IGNATIUS CHASUBLE
1250 x 740mm
***Circa* 1650-1670**

Little is known about the early history of this beautiful seventeenth-century chasuble. It is of English design, and the embroiderer was clearly well acquainted with the Jesuits, as the front and back of the vestment bear images of St Ignatius Loyola (*circa* 1491-1556), the founder of the Society of Jesus, and of St Francis Xavier (1506-1552), the famous Jesuit missionary.

The rector of Stonyhurst bought the chasuble at an auction in 1835, but there are no clues as to its whereabouts before that date. Many Catholic families started to bring treasured vestments out of hiding about that time, after Catholic Relief Acts, gradually easing the condition of Catholics, were passed by parliament in 1778, 1791 and 1829.

3.6

79

3.7

THE WINTOUR WHITE CHASUBLE
Silk brocade, silk threads, gold thread, semi-precious stones, 1120 x 640mm
Circa 1655
Loaned by the British Province of the Society of Jesus

This beautiful chasuble has a deeply romantic history. It is one of several sets of vestments made in the mid-seventeenth century by Helena Wintour (*circa* 1600-1671), whose name can be seen embroidered in the circlet at the bottom of the chasuble. Helena's father was Robert Wintour, who, along with two of his brothers, became embroiled in the Gunpowder Plot with Guy Fawkes and Robert Catesby in 1605. When the Plot failed, all three brothers died, either during capture or on the scaffold as traitors. Helena was about five years old at this time.

Helena's family was left largely without protection or income, and in time most of them emigrated to join the many English Catholics in exile on the continent. She, however, stayed behind, on the family farm in Worcestershire, where she spent the remainder of her long life praying, fasting, doing charitable works and making beautiful embroidered vestments. Her skill as a needlewoman is evident, and in addition to the beautiful silks and gold threads used in the design, she also sewed in semi-precious jewels and pearls from her own jewellery box. She was a great supporter of the clandestine missionary work carried out by the Jesuits in Worcester, and made generous promises to assist them in her will. She died without formally making a will, but there is a document in the Stonyhurst Archives signed in her own hand on the day of her death that makes her intentions clear:

> I do also leave and bequeath unto the said Society [of Jesus] all the vestments and other altar ornaments thereto belonging whereof I am at present possessed. Given under my hand this fifth day of May, one thousand six hundred and seventy one. All this I declare as part of my will and testament.

The document was immediately contested by Helena's niece by marriage, Lady Wintour, who coveted the magnificent vestments, and the ensuing row threatened to expose the Jesuits, who were working in secret owing to the laws forbidding Catholic priests from working in England. To settle the matter, the Jesuits gave Lady Wintour two of the four best vestments. Little is known about the sets that remained in their possession until about 1820 when they were discovered in a chest in the attic of Grafton Manor in Worcestershire. In 1854 they were sent to Stonyhurst where they received much-needed restoration.

The design on the back of the chasuble

3.7

shows the vision of the Lamb on the Altar from the Book of the Apocalypse. It is surrounded by carnations, roses, tulips, pomegranates and other fruits and flowers, which all symbolise aspects of Christ's life, death and resurrection, or qualities attributed to Mary, His Mother. The embroidered words *Alleluia, alleluia, alleluia,* make this chasuble particularly appropriate for use on Easter Sunday.

3.8
THE WINTOUR RED CHALICE VEIL
600 x 600mm
Circa 1660
Loaned by the British Province of the Society of Jesus

This chalice veil is part of a set of red vestments embroidered by Helena Wintour, of which now only it and the chasuble remain. The fabric is rich silk velvet decorated with gold lace, and embroidered motifs representing the Dove of the Holy Spirit, and the tongues of fire and mighty rushing wind that descended on the first apostles at Pentecost.

3.8

3.9

ST WINEFRIDE'S CHALICE VEIL

550 x 570mm

Circa 1610-1640

This elaborately embroidered chalice veil dates from the mid-seventeenth century and was made as a thanksgiving following a miraculous cure at St Winefride's Well at Holywell in north Wales. The Well has been a place of pilgrimage since the early Middle Ages, when the water that flows from an underground spring was credited with healing properties. St Winefride (*circa* 600-660) was a Welsh princess who fled her home to avoid a forced marriage to a pagan nobleman, Caradoc. He followed her and murdered her, cutting off her head. A spring of water appeared on the spot where her head hit the ground. Her uncle, St Beuno (*d.* 660), a holy priest who lived nearby, restored Winefride to life. In her picture on the veil, the red line around her throat indicates where her head was joined back onto her body.

Pilgrims visited the Well in great numbers. Henry V, in 1416, and, later, Katherine of Aragon, the wife of Henry VIII, went on pilgrimage to Holywell. Even during the Reformation and the persecution of the sixteenth and seventeenth centuries, pilgrims continued to visit Holywell clandestinely. James II and Mary of Modena went on pilgrimage there in 1686.

The veil bears the name of Maria Bodenham, a member of the famous Catholic recusant family. She made it to record her family's gratitude after her father-in-law, Sir Roger Bodenham (1545-1623), of Rotherwas, near Hereford, was cured of a leg ailment at the Well in 1606.

3.9

De la Grappe qu'on à
trouvé dans le Scapu-
laire du Cimetière
Sobieski Reine
D'Angleterre après sa
Mort, tout penetré
de sa Sueur

Linge qu...

Ex Carne
accepi à

K.
a Pir
...

Lewis Card.
Barroni

Jacobi 2ᵢ Regis.
P. Hen: Humberston.

of yᵉ Blood of
King James yᵉ 2

h. haire &

of his Flesh

Jacobitism: An Introduction

LEO GOOCH

*J*acobus is the Latin form of the name James, from which the term *Jacobitism* is derived. Jacobites were those who sought the restoration to the English throne and royal succession of:

- the Catholic king, James II (1633-1701), overthrown in 1688 by the Protestant William of Orange;
- his son, James Francis Edward (1688-1766), titular King James III, known as the *Old Pretender;*
- James II's grandson, Charles Edward (1720-1788), the *Bonnie Prince* or *Young Pretender.*

The exiled Jacobite court was established first at St Germain-en-Laye, to the west of Paris, under the protection of the French kings, and subsequently on papal territory in Italy. Though Jacobitism is often thought of as a Scottish phenomenon, it gained a wide appeal in England, Wales and Ireland. Indeed, as the regime of William of Orange increasingly gave offence to many sections of society, the Jacobite movement attracted considerable support throughout Britain within the major religious denominations and political parties. The close association between the Stuarts and Catholicism, however, meant that a restoration could not be effected politically, but only as the result of a successful military campaign. In the sixty years following the revolution of 1688, several risings and armed engagements took place. It is through them, therefore, that the history of the Jacobite cause has to be told.

The Scottish Jacobites were victorious in the Battle of Killiecrankie in July 1689, but they were defeated at Dunkeld the following year. Defeats in the Battle of the Boyne in 1690 and in the Battle of Aughrim in 1691 put paid to James's hopes in Ireland. With 'Celtic Jacobitism' in disarray, the French were asked to come to James's aid with a cross-Channel invasion in 1692, but the fleet was defeated in the Battle of La Hogue. In 1695 a second enterprise was abandoned. In 1708 a third Franco-Jacobite insurgency was launched, this time to land a force in the Firth of Forth to exploit Scottish resentment over the Act of Union of 1707, but that was repulsed. From then onwards, the French would accept only a minimal role in Jacobite military operations.

Attention shifted to northern England and this appeared to be strategically sound for several reasons. In the first place, the majority of English Catholics desired a restoration of the Stuarts to the throne. Since most of them lived in the northern counties, it was anticipated that the landing of an invading force there would attract greatest support. Secondly, those Scots who remained loyal to James II would be able to join their English counterparts easily. Thirdly, the industrial north could quickly bring London to a standstill, particularly if coal supplies from Tyneside to the capital were cut in good time. This was the theory on which the Jacobite rising of 1715 was based.

An action plan was formulated to assemble an Anglo-Scottish army in Northumberland, reinforced by exiled Jacobites from France. Together, they were to seize Newcastle and seal off the Tyne, thereby bringing coal shipments to London to a halt. They then planned to sweep south to take the capital, joined on the way by large and increasing numbers of followers.

As events turned out, the execution of the plan was botched. Problems of co-ordination and communication arose from the start and the planned landing of Jacobites from France did not take place. The Jacobite leaders – the Anglican MP, Thomas Forster, and the Catholic Earl of Derwentwater, James Radcliffe, of Dilston in Northumberland – were unqualified for military command. To the dismay of the Scots, the predicted extent of English support for the rising did not materialise – and government forces were unexpectedly loyal and strong. Instead of having an easy and jubilant march down the Great North Road to London, the Jacobites were compelled to turn north to join their Scottish allies and then to seek greater assistance in Cumbria and Lancashire.

The extent of Catholicism and Jacobitism in the north-west of England was particularly marked and allegations of anti-government plots had abounded since the revolution of 1688. In 1694 the supposed conspirators, including many leading Catholics, were brought to trial in Manchester, only to be acquitted because the prosecution evidence was shown to be perjured. At the time of the Jacobite rising in 1715, however, it was said that some twenty thousand men in the region were impatient to take to arms on James's side. In that year, the Anglo-Scottish Jacobite insurgent force made its way south from the western Scottish borders. There was general dismay when only around fifteen hundred Lancastrians came out to give their support. Fatally, the Jacobites paused too long at Preston where they were surrounded and were forced to surrender. A concurrent Scottish campaign petered out in January 1716 at Perth.

The government acted quickly to stamp out English Jacobitism. The principal leaders were executed, others were imprisoned, and many rank and file Jacobites were banished to the colonies. The real estate of the rebels was confiscated. To the extent that hardly a Northumbrian Catholic took to Jacobite arms again, the policy succeeded. However, the Jacobite cause was not defeated.

In 1717, James turned for help to certain continental countries hostile to Britain. A plan for a joint Swedish and Russian invasion of Scotland was thwarted when the British government learned of it. In 1719, Spain, now at war with England, assembled an armada at Cadiz to invade England and Scotland simultaneously. But the fleet bound for England encountered severe storms and most of the ships were lost. Although the men bound for Scotland made a landing, they were cornered at Glenshiel and annihilated. A quarter of a century would pass before the Jacobites ventured out again – this time under the personal command of Prince Charles – known among his followers as *Bonnie Prince Charlie*.

On 19 August 1745 the Jacobite standard was raised at Glenfinnan. Charles took Perth and Edinburgh with little difficulty and he won a resounding victory over the Hanoverian army at Prestonpans on 21 September. Now, Scotland was effectively a Stuart kingdom once more and an invasion of England became inevitable. In a tactically faultless advance, Charles marched southwards, taking Carlisle, Lancaster, Preston and Manchester. However, the long hoped-for widespread support from England did not materialise: the only substantial English contribution was that of Colonel Charles Towneley, a Catholic, whose Manchester Regiment of some three hundred men joined forces on the way.

Remarkably, the Jacobites remained unopposed and by the beginning of December 1745 they reached Derby, just one hundred and twenty miles from London. It was at this point, however, that the Scottish commanders lost their nerve: they felt exposed, they were uncertain of the location and condition of the government's forces, and they lacked confirmation of a complementary cross-Channel invasion by the French. Ignoring the prince's entreaties to press on, they insisted on retreat: with that, the best chance of a Stuart restoration was lost.

The return of the main force to Scotland was accomplished without incident, except for a short skirmish with the Duke of Cumberland's vanguard at Clifton, south of Penrith. The Manchester Regiment, however, acting as rearguard at Carlisle was forced to surrender. Towneley and eight of his officers were executed. The Scottish Jacobites won an engagement at Falkirk, but by then they had lost heart in the campaign. A few low-level encounters followed during a progressive withdrawal into the Highlands before the two armies faced each other on Culloden Moor on 16 April 1746 in what would be their last trial of arms. The dispirited and exhausted Jacobites were destroyed in less than an hour.

Numbers of Jacobites managed to evade capture and escape to France, although it would be five months before Prince Charles could be got safely out of Scotland. As was to be expected, large numbers of executions, imprisonments, transportations and sequestrations of property followed.

Most of the Jacobite risings had little chance of success but the *Forty-five*, as it came to be known, was close-run. The Duke of Cumberland, for one, certainly understood that it had been a greater threat to the Hanoverian regime than could be admitted: in a reign of terror in which he savagely and ruthlessly dispossessed and dissolved the Highland clans, he did his level best to eliminate the possibility of another uprising. Nonetheless, for several years afterwards some feared that the Jacobites might rise again. In reality, the long intermittent military campaign to restore the Stuarts to the three kingdoms of England, Scotland and Ireland had come to an end.

The Jacobites at the highest level were nothing if not persistent in trying to bring about a restoration of the Stuarts to the throne, but theirs was a peculiarly unfortunate movement. In one way or another, every one of their planned risings was bedevilled by bad weather, particularly during winter campaigning, indecisive leadership, poor coordination and communications, or changing diplomatic alliances on the continent. But perhaps the greatest single factor was the over-estimation of the willingness of English Jacobites actually to take to arms. The Scottish Jacobites were certainly fed extravagant estimates of the numbers of men who would turn out. When they did not, discussions among the leaders became acrimonious and made the conduct of operations in 1715 and 1745 fearful and timid.

The Stuart dynasty was not blessed with great success in England in the two centuries between the execution of Mary, Queen of Scots, in 1587 and the death of 'Charles III' in 1788. Both of their claims to the English throne went unfulfilled, but the latter suffered the further indignity of having his royal status withdrawn by the Holy See at the death of his father in 1766. The direct line came to an end at the death in 1807 of Henry Benedict Stuart, Cardinal Duke of York (1725-1807), recognised by his Jacobite followers as 'Henry IX'.

*Lock of hair of Prince Charles Edward Stuart,
included in a case containing his miniature portrait
(see 4.7, p. 104).*

4.1

LOCKET CONTAINING THE HAIR OF MARY, QUEEN OF SCOTS (1542-1587)
Silver case, glass, velvet and human hair, 78 x 60mm
1568 (?)

There is no proof that this lock of hair belonged to Mary Stuart, nor is there any documentation to back up the claim that it was bestowed by her on George Douglas in return for his assistance in helping her to escape incarceration in Lochleven Castle in 1568. However, claims such as these that run in families for generations very often have some grounding in truth.

The locket contains hair of a distinct auburn shade, which tallies with contemporary descriptions of Mary Stuart's colouring and with portraits of her. Interestingly, it is similar, though slightly darker, to the hair in the locket in this exhibition which came from the head of her great-great-great-great-grandson, Prince Charles Edward Stuart.

Mary Stuart's history was turbulent and marked with tragedy and high drama. The circumstances in which this lock of hair was given are typical of her life story. On returning to Scotland a widow in 1560, her religion, her first marriage to Lord Darnley, her suspected complicity in his murder and her subsequent marriage to the man thought most likely to have had a hand in his death combined to provoke a revolt amongst her people and the nobility. Defeated in battle, Mary was held prisoner in Lochleven Castle – an ancient keep entirely surrounded by water – and forced to abdicate in favour of her infant son. She prevailed upon the youthful son of her captor, George Douglas, to assist her to escape, leaving him with this lock of hair as a grateful souvenir.

Mary's status amongst Catholics after her execution was ambiguous. Many saw her as a martyr for the Catholic faith, and items associated with her were highly sought after. Books, dress fabrics, embroideries and locks of hair all were collected and treasured as a link with the martyr queen. The Stuart dynasty's tragic and romantic existence, and their eventual expulsion from the British Isles because of their Catholic faith, ensured an eager audience for relics such as this lock of hair.

4.1

95

COPE AND CHASUBLE FROM THE PORTUGUESE EMBASSY CHAPEL, LONDON
1150 x 670mm
Circa **1670-1730**

During penal times in England and Wales, when Catholics were forbidden to attend Mass, there were only two options open to those who wished to practise their faith. Catholics could either attend secret Masses said by missionary priests who moved around the country, or were based in remote rural houses, or they could attend the London Catholic chapels attached to the embassies of Catholic countries such as Spain and Portugal.

As these chapels were located within diplomatic premises, the laws observed there were those of the embassy's home country.

Some of these chapels sponsored and commissioned music from eminent composers, and attracted famous Catholic musicians from continental Europe to perform in London: as such they became fashionable, even among non-Catholics.

The cope and chasuble shown here are part of a large group of vestments in many different liturgical colours purchased by Stonyhurst College in 1835 when the Portuguese Embassy Chapel in London closed, following new laws which allowed Catholic public worship in England once more.

4.2

4.3

THE EASTER MISSAL OF JAMES II
Leather and gilt stamped binding, 190 x 220mm
No publication date, presumed *circa* 1690-1700

This small but handsome book is part of a group of volumes which originally belonged to James II (1633-1701) and his family. The binding bears the arms of the king, and, on the inside front cover hidden under nineteenth-century endpapers is the inscription – *Le Roy d'Angletair* (The King of England). This inscription was discovered in the late nineteenth century when the book was inadvertently left by its previous owner on a window sill during a shower of rain. The book became damp and the marbled endpaper peeled away revealing the inscription in James II's hand underneath.

James II, his wife and baby son were forced to flee from England in December 1688 when the country was invaded from the Netherlands by a force led by William of Orange (1650-1702), who had married James's daughter, Mary, in 1677. James was a convert to Catholicism, a fact which had caused much uneasiness in Britain when he became king on the death of his brother, Charles II, in 1685. His two daughters from his first marriage were, however, Protestant, and people were therefore assured that the succession would revert to the Church of England on James's death.

James married again in 1673. His new wife was an Italian Catholic princess, Mary Beatrice of Modena (1658-1718). Over a period of fifteen years, the couple produced ten children who either died at birth or shortly thereafter. The birth in 1688 of James, a healthy child, who would take precedence over Mary and Anne, provoked the invasion of William of Orange, and, as a result, James lost his throne and took refuge in France.

This book dates from the time when James set up a rival court in exile under the protection of Louis XIV of France at the Château of St Germain-en-Laye.

4.3

4.4

FRAGMENTS OF HAIR, FLESH AND CLOTHING OF JAMES II

Human hair, skin, blood, linen and wool flannel, 330 x 410 x 90mm

1701

The medieval practice of donating parts of royal corpses to favoured individuals was continued into the eighteenth century. It had its origins in the belief that kings were divinely appointed by God, and that their mortal remains therefore had some religious significance over and above those of ordinary people.

Before his death, James specified who should be the recipients of various parts of his anatomy. When he succumbed to a cerebral haemorrhage in 1701, his brain was sent to the Scots College in Paris, his heart to a convent at Chaillot, half of his bowels to the English College at St Omers, and the remainder of his intestines were buried in a lead chest in the parish church at St Germain-en-Laye. James II had been a great benefactor to St Omers during his lifetime, donating many ancient sets of vestments, as well as a magnificent new set of cloth of gold vestments, which still survive at Stonyhurst.

James's body was encased in a lead coffin and transferred to the church of the English Benedictines in Paris where it was to await the time when it could be taken to Westminster Abbey and buried among his ancestors. That was not to be: the body was desecrated and lost during the French Revolution, along with the remains at the Scots College, Chaillot and St Omers. The lead case at St Germain survived and can still be seen today.

It is likely that these small fragments of greying hair, unidentified flesh, blood-soaked cloth and flannel were sent to St Omers at approximately the same time as the gift of the bowels. The three manuscript labels identifying them appear to date from the early eighteenth century. The text reads:

> Ex carne Jacobi 2d Regis accepi a P. Hen Humberston/ K.J. haire & a Piece of his flesh also a Piece of ye Flanell wastcoate he dyed in/Of ye Blood of King James ye 2d.

Fr Henry Humberston (1638-1708) had been a pupil at St Omers before joining the Society of Jesus in 1658. He worked as a missionary in Worcester during the reign of James II. In 1701 he was finishing a four-year term of office as provincial superior of the English Jesuits, and moved to take up the post of rector of St Omers in that same year. It is highly likely that he received these small relics of the dead king when he was provincial superior and donated them to St Omers.

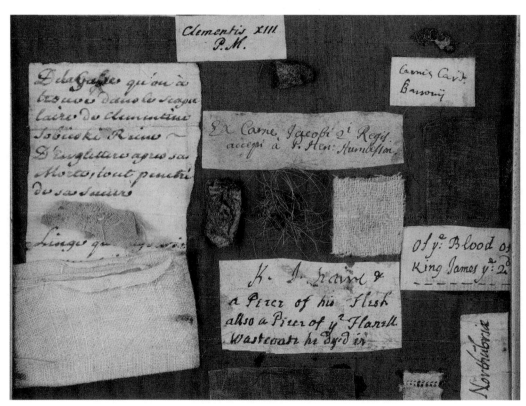

4.4

4.5 and 4.6
MINIATURE BROOCHES OF JAMES III AND CLEMENTINA SOBIESKA STUART
Watercolour on ivory, crystal and silver gilt mounting
Circa 1720-1730

These two small brooches form a natural pair, although they are not identical and may not have been made at the same time. They depict James III (1688-1766), also known as the Old Pretender, and his wife Princess Maria Clementina Sobieska (1702-1735).

James was the eleventh child born to his parents, James II of England and Queen Mary Beatrice, but the first to survive beyond infancy. His birth provoked a rebellion amongst English Protestants fearful of a new Catholic monarchy, and when he was barely seven weeks old Prince James and his mother escaped from England and went into exile in France, whence they were shortly followed by James II.

James became king in 1701 at the age of thirteen. Although he was recognised as the rightful king by the courts of France, Spain, Modena and by the papacy, he was never crowned or even set foot in England during his lifetime. He made two unsuccessful attempts to regain the throne in 1708 and in 1715, when he succeeded in landing in Scotland, but he was driven out after a month.

He married Clementina Sobieska in 1719; she was seventeen and he was thirty-one. She was a great heiress, and the couple were treated by most of Europe as the king and queen of England. They lived in some style, supported by her wealth and also by numerous pensions and bequests donated by well-wishers and political allies. However the marriage was not altogether happy. The couple had two healthy children, Charles and Henry, who both grew into adulthood, but in 1727 Clementina left James for a convent, claiming that he was an adulterer. After two years she was reconciled, but her physical and mental health had deteriorated and she died in 1735 at the age of thirty-three.

These small brooches were designed to be worn by Jacobite sympathisers. They would have been seen as unwise indicators of Jacobite allegiance during the eighteenth century, but, in the Victorian era, the romantic nature of the Stuart story made it highly popular and these brooches would then have become desirable fashion items.

4.5 and 4.6

4.7

MINIATURE OF PRINCE CHARLES EDWARD STUART
Watercolour and varnish on ivory, human hair, 90 x 70mm
Circa 1737-1750

This oval frame contains not only a miniature of Prince Charles Edward Stuart (1720-1788) as a young man, probably aged between seventeen and thirty, but also a lock of reddish gold hair claimed to be his. An engraved inscription round the edge of the frame reads:

Part of lock of Prince Charles Edward's hair sent by Dr Watson to Rev Bury. Cut in 1737 when about 17.

Neither Dr Watson nor the Reverend Mr Bury have been reliably identified, which raises a question as to the provenance of the lock of hair. The date claimed for the hair is, however, quite specific, which helps to lend it authenticity. There was a vibrant trade in Jacobite 'relics' in the eighteenth century amongst supporters and sympathisers of the Stuart cause, many of whom were simply carried along by the romantic nature of the Prince's cause.

In the portrait miniature, Prince Charles is shown in armour, as was traditional with royal portraits, emphasising not only the sitter's bravery and valour in battle, but also his role as commander-in-chief of the country's armed forces. In fact Prince Charles first saw military action at the age of fourteen at the Siege of Gaeta in 1734. In 1743 Charles's father, known to the Jacobite cause as King James III and VIII (1688-1766), and to the Hanoverians as the Old Pretender, declared his son to be Prince Regent, thereby crediting him with the authority to re-establish the British throne in his own right in the forthcoming planned invasion.

4.7

4.8

FRAGMENT OF TARTAN WORN BY PRINCE CHARLES EDWARD STUART
Wool and various vegetable and animal dyes, 100 x 90mm
Circa 1745

This small and much-darkened piece of fabric was once part of a plaid suit worn briefly by Prince Charles Edward Stuart (1720-1788), otherwise known as *Bonnie Prince Charlie,* during his desperate flight to France after defeat at the battle of Culloden on 16 April 1746.

It came to Stonyhurst in the early twentieth century, but it was only in the 1980s that research proved its authenticity. Accompanying the fabric is a nineteenth-century label which reads:

> This piece of cloth is part of a kilt left by Prince Charlie in the House of Campbell, Island of Glass, 30th April 1746. Robert Hemsley, Tarber House, got it from a descendant of Campbell's and sent it to Walter Armstrong of Tarff House, Kirkcowan, who gave it to J. S. Maitland, 19th April 1887. In landing on the island Prince Charlie got wet. His kilt was not dry in the morning when he wished to start so he left his own behind and took one of Campbell's kilts.

Original eye-witness accounts taken from those involved in the rebellion and its aftermath confirm this story. In 1747, the Jacobite annalist, Robert Forbes (*bap.* 1708-1775), subsequently Scottish Episcopal Bishop of Ross and Caithness, travelled the Highlands taking depositions from Prince Charles's companions and recorded numerous first-hand accounts of the Prince's flight. According to him, Angus Macdonald was the laird of Borrodale and the owner of the house which sheltered the sodden Prince. It was his plaid which was given to the fugitive by his wife, Catriona, so that he "might better pass for one of the country".

The following day, Prince Charles, wearing the Borrodale plaid, moved on to his next place of refuge, and again was soaked in the crossing to Eilean Glas (or *Island of Glass,* as described literally on the original label), where Donald Campbell gave him sanctuary. Here Prince Charles was given further dry clothes and he left behind the wet plaid belonging to Angus Macdonald. This was cut into pieces for souvenirs, of which only three fragments now remain – this being one of them.

The wool has been identified as originating from a Highland breed of sheep, and the dyes are all consistent with those used in the mid-eighteenth century. Stonyhurst College has recreated the pattern and named it *Lady Borrodale's Gift,* and it is now worn by the girls at the College as part of their school uniform.

4.8

4.9

CANTUS DIVERSI
Manuscript by John Francis Wade, 190 x 300mm
1751

John Francis Wade (1711/12–1786) was a Latin teacher and choirmaster at the English College, Douai, the Catholic seminary for English and Welsh priests in northern France, founded in 1568 by Cardinal William Allen (1532-1594), who was born at Rossall in the Fylde area of Lancashire.

Wade supplemented his teaching income by copying church music, and produced this book of Mass settings and other sacred songs, presumably for use by the choir at Douai. Its title means *diverse,* or *various songs.* At the end of the book, Wade added a composition of his own, a short Latin carol which he entitled *Adeste Fideles (O come, all ye faithful).*

Wade is thought to have based his tune on an old English air, and its popularity spread rapidly. It became known in London through performances at the Catholic embassy chapels, and was spread through England and Scotland by travelling missionary priests. Soon, according to contemporary reports, "apprentice boys whistled it in every street, and even the blackbirds joined in the chorus".

This is the oldest known version of the hymn. There are four other manuscript copies in existence but all are dated later, or are undated.

níte, veníte in Béthlehem. * Natum vidéte

Regem Angelórum: veníte, adorémus: ℟.Ve-

níte, adorémus: veníte, adorémus Dóminum.

Deum de Deo, lumen de lúmine, geſtant

Puéllæ víſcera: * Deum verum, génitum non

factum: veníte, adorémus: ℟.Veníte, adoré-

mus: veníte, adorémus Dóminum. Cantet

nunc i o chorus Angelórum, cantet nunc

aula cæléſtium, Glória in excélſis Deo:

veníte, adorémus ℟. Veníte, adorémus: ve-

níte, adorémus Dóminum. Ergo qui natus

die hodiérna, Jeſu tibi ſit glória. * Pa-

tris ætérni Verbum caro factum: veníte a-

dorémus: Veníte, adorémus: veníte, adoré-

mus Dóminum. 6.

Puer nobis naſcitur, Rectórque Ange-

lórum: In hoc mundo paſcitur Dóminus do-

minórum. In Præſepe po   ſub fæno aſinó-
                                        rum

4.9

4.10

MINIATURE OF PRINCE CHARLES EDWARD STUART IN LATER LIFE
Watercolour and varnish on ivory
Circa 1770

On the back of this miniature is a contemporary manuscript note that reads:

> P" C" Very good likeness in 1770 attest by Henry Crathorne Esqr often on his travels and frequently in his company.

In 1770, Prince Charles (1720-1788) was a disappointed man, alienated from the Catholic Church and embittered that his claim to the British throne in 1766 on the death of his father, James III and VIII (1688-1766), had not been officially recognised by the pope, or the kings of France and Spain, and indeed that they had recognised the Hanoverian succession as valid. He had a number of mistresses and two illegitimate children, and, following the failure of the 1745 rebellion, he took to drinking heavily.

The face of the Prince in this miniature differs greatly from the earlier painting: the effects of alcohol and unwise living are clearly visible in his features.

In 1772 he married Princess Louise Stolberg-Gedern (1752-1824), who was thirty-two years his junior, but the union was not a success. She claimed that he physically abused her, and eventually separated from Prince Charles to live with the Italian dramatist Count Vittorio Alfieri (1752-1803).

Prince Charles died in 1788 and is buried in St Peter's in Rome.

Henry Crathorne came from a Catholic Yorkshire family and is almost certainly identical with the "Sir Henry Crathorn of York" who registered as a student at the Collegio dei Nobili di San Francesco Saverio at Bologna in May 1772 and then at the Collegio San Carlo at Modena in August 1773 as part of his grand tour of Italy. It also seems likely that he is the same Mr Crathorne who arrived in Rome in the autumn of 1774 accompanied by a former student of St Omers, Father William Meynell SJ (1744-1826), before spending the winter moving between Rome and Naples. Prince Charles had a wide circle of companions: from the surviving evidence, Crathorne was one of these.

Crathorne's movements in Italy are recorded in the surviving letters of the Halifax-born English Jesuit, Father John Thorpe (1726-1792), another former student of St Omers, who lived in Rome from 1756 until his death.

It is not clear how the miniature passed into the hands of the Society of Jesus. However, it was presented to Stonyhurst in 1842 by the Lancashire-born provincial

4.10

superior of the English Jesuits, Father Randal Lythgoe (1793-1855), who opened the new Jesuit day school of St Francis Xavier in Liverpool that year.

The Nineteenth-Century Gothic Revival: Stonyhurst and the Link with Liverpool

ANTHONY SYMONDSON SJ

Early in the nineteenth century, the Gothic Revival, previously associated with a romantic interest in medieval forms and whims, took a new course and became closely identified with a religious revival. This was Catholic in origin but came to transform the church architecture of the Victorian age and included buildings of all types. The change was entirely due to one man, Augustus Welby Northmore Pugin (1812-1852). In 1834, three years before the accession of Queen Victoria, the twenty-three-year-old Pugin wrote to his friend, William Osmund, in laconic terms:

> I can assure you after a close and impartial investigation I feel perfectly convinced the roman Catholick church is the only true one – and the only one in which the grand & sublime style of church architecture can ever be restored – A very big chapel is now building in the north & when compleat I certainly think I shall recant. I know you will blame me but I am internally convinced – that it is right.

In 1829 the Catholic Relief Act was passed, enabling the Catholic community to worship freely for the first time in three hundred years. Almost all disabilities were removed and Catholics were admitted to most public offices. They were put on the same basis of equality with non-Catholics and were given the same civil rights. The architectural prospects for building new churches, convents, monasteries and schools were bright, as implied by the oblique reference to "a very big chapel ... now building in the north". The chapel in question was the collegiate church of St Peter, Stonyhurst, designed by the Catholic architect, Joseph John Scoles (1798-1863). It is a fine building erected by the Jesuits between 1832 and 1835 in the Perpendicular style, influenced in the exterior elevations by King's College Chapel, Cambridge. In style it complements the fine sixteenth-century mansion or "prodigy house", fit to entertain a king or queen, built at Stonyhurst by Sir Richard Shireburn between 1590 and 1606. Scoles went on to complete the main façade of the house in the 1840s, as well as the infirmary wing to its left, with its tall, terracotta chimneys complementing the turrets of the church opposite.

Pugin later visited Stonyhurst and designed two stained glass windows for the church. But Scoles's Gothic was subtly different from his. In 1836 Pugin leapt to fame when he published *Contrasts,* a plea for Catholicism illustrated by brilliant comparisons between the meanness, cruelty and vulgarity of buildings of his own day – Classical or minimum Gothic – and the glories of the Catholic past. In 1841 he wrote a more detailed and closely considered book, *The True Principles of Pointed or Christian Architecture,* and showed a deeper understanding than anyone before of the connections between Gothic style and structure and the function of each member. In this and later books, Pugin rediscovered the structural logic of Gothic architecture. His buildings assumed the constructional conviction and building methods of the medieval past and his churches were liturgically planned and furnished on medievalist principles. Pugin's faith and his architectural ideals were one.

Pugin not only revived authentic Gothic design, but also went on to revitalize medieval techniques in precious and base metalwork, embroidery, woodwork and stone-carving, tile-making and stained glass. Working with John Hardman (1811-1867), a Birmingham button-maker who had been educated at Stonyhurst from 1824 to 1827, Pugin's medieval manufactures came to furnish hundreds of Catholic and Anglican churches for the rest of the nineteenth century and beyond. The Church of England was transformed by the Anglo-Catholic principles of the Oxford Movement and extensive church-building activity resulted, leaving few regions of Britain untouched. But to no other architect does Victorian church design owe

more than to Pugin. The workmanship to be found in most Victorian churches is the fruit of his experiments.

Scoles's architectural range was broader than Pugin's. His domestic architecture was Classical and his churches were also designed in the Romanesque and Classical styles. The church at Stonyhurst is stiffer and thinner than Pugin's work and Scoles provoked Pugin's scorn when he designed St John's, Duncan Terrace, Islington, London, between 1841 and 1843 in the Romanesque style with Classical fittings. But in his later work Scoles learnt from *True Principles* and these are reflected in two Jesuit churches – St Francis Xavier's, Liverpool (1845-8), and, even more strongly, in the London church of the Immaculate Conception, Farm Street, Mayfair (1846-9). Pugin designed the high altar at Farm Street and his disciple, Thomas Earley, executed the fine hanging rood cross at St Francis Xavier's. Throughout both churches, the influence of Pugin is to be found in the wealth of stone sculpture, altar plate, tiles and stained glass.

This endeavour in Liverpool culminated in Edmund Kirby's sumptuous chapel, built in 1884-7 for the parish sodalities, or religious guilds for men, women and children, formed for devotions and good works. They were the centres of the church's Catholic life and activity. The Sodality Chapel at St Francis Xavier's, today separated from the main body of the church by a glazed screen, is almost a church within a church and its decoration continued until 1893. The symbolism of the rich sculpture – some of it executed by Conrad Dressler, of Chelsea, London – and of the stained glass within the Sodality Chapel is confined to scenes from the lives of the Virgin Mary and many Jesuit saints.

Stonyhurst also has a fine Sodality Chapel, designed by Charles Alban Buckler (1824–1905), and opened in 1859. Tall and narrow, the walls and roof were originally decorated in Puginian painted patterns. "We have seen nothing in the North of England," declared the Preston historian, Anthony Hewitson, in 1878, "equal to this chapel in sweetness and compactness of design, in richness of colouring, excellence of finish, and costliness of workmanship". In Liverpool only the ceiling of the nave of St Francis Xavier's was decorated in gold and colour. These features were unfortunately lost in 1948 when serious war damage to the roof of the church necessitated the complete removal of the original ceiling.

There is relatively little in the Stonyhurst collections that belongs to the Gothic Revival. Scoles's Bay Library at Stonyhurst contains an almost complete set of Pugin's publications, including the *Glossary of Ecclesiastical Ornament and Costume* and *Floriated Ornament,* both brilliantly illustrated by chromolithographic plates executed in heraldic colour. Many were presented by Pugin's great-grandson, Father Philip Watts SJ (1883-1943), who taught at Stonyhurst for many years and who was curator of the collections there. For Father Watts's first Mass, his family presented to him a splendid set of white Low Mass vestments, made from his mother's wedding dress, which he bequeathed to Stonyhurst. Though these are in the Latin shape, they provide a direct link with Pugin as the father of the Gothic Revival as their embroidery shows the influence of medieval stitching. Pugin's principles would not have been diffused without his powerful writings. They enflamed the imagination of young architects and their patrons and the books at Stonyhurst referred to, coming from Pugin's family, are a strong link with his mind and influence.

The Catholic Revival in England went hand-in-hand with the revival of Catholic history. Pugin was influenced by the research into medieval liturgy and ceremonial undertaken by the Liverpool-born Daniel Rock (1799-1871), domestic chaplain to Lord Shrewsbury. The leading English Catholic historian of the nineteenth-century was Dr John Lingard (1771-1851), a priest of great learning who spent most of his life in the north of England, looking after the rural parish of Hornby, in the Lune valley, from 1811 until his death forty years later. Born in Winchester in 1771 to Catholic parents from Claxby in Lincolnshire, Lingard inherited from "stock winnowed and strengthened by the ceaseless oppression of two centuries the silent, stubborn, almost sullen longing for the conversion of his native land, that is so intimate a characteristic of the pre-

Emancipation Catholic". In 1819 he published the first of three volumes of a *History of England* and these continued until the publication of the eighth volume in 1830. Founded on wide research in original documents, Lingard's *History* is noted for its unbiased accuracy and as a "sober, unimpassioned statement of incontrovertible fact". Lingard's work as a historian changed the national understanding of history and the role of the Catholic Church in its chronicles.

The nineteenth century marked the height of Britain's world leadership and economic power. During the progress of the Gothic Revival, the face of Britain was changed. The Gothic style was not simply confined to churches. Domestic architecture, civil and railway architecture, factories and warehouses were built in the Gothic style and for a time Britain broke new frontiers in architecture. From it grew the Domestic Revival, the Pre-Raphaelite, Arts and Crafts and Aesthetic Movements, and many other developments in art and architecture. This was reflected at Stonyhurst in 1876-89 when the Catholic architects, Dunn & Hansom, built the long range of the south wing. This became known as New Stonyhurst. Strongly influenced in style by the Elizabethan mansion of the Shireburn family, the wing is a brilliant synthesis of the Renaissance and late-Gothic styles blended into unity. At the centre is the Academy Room where the school assembles and, to the west, the Perpendicular Gothic Boys' Chapel with a wooden vault and a

towering wooden altar-screen containing scenes from the life of St Aloysius Gonzaga, the school's patron, painted by Percy Bacon. New Stonyhurst comprises the best school buildings of their date in Britain. Less disciplined in design, Kirby's Sodality Chapel in Liverpool is a counterpart to this endeavour. Kirby went on to design a polychromatic high altar of marble for the church at Stonyhurst and, after the First World War, he designed a memorial chapel at the end of one of the school's galleries containing a fine bas-relief by Gilbert Ledward (1888-1960).

The Gothic Revival effectively came to an end with the Great War. After 1918 there were no longer the economic resources to maintain it and a new generation preferred stripped Classicism or made a clean break with the past by embracing the Modern Movement. It continued in church architecture, as Sir Giles Gilbert Scott's monumental Liverpool Cathedral triumphantly demonstrates. At Stonyhurst, the Perpendicular Gothic Rhetoric Wing, designed by J. Armes of Darlington, was opened in 1965. Built of stone from a demolished Gothic Revival bank and Methodist chapel, it contains doors and panelling designed by Alfred Waterhouse in 1870-83 for Eaton Hall, near Chester, the mid-Victorian Gothic seat of the Duke of Westminster, which was demolished in 1961.

But of all the exhibits from Stonyhurst associated with the Gothic Revival, there is one that has links with the medieval past and the Old Faith in a way that would have delighted the heart of Pugin. A red silk chasuble has exquisitely embroidered orphreys taken from a vestment made in the late Middle Ages for use in Westminster Abbey. It is mounted on lustrous silk damask designed by Sir Ninian Comper (1864-1960), the leading church architect of the late-nineteenth and early-twentieth centuries. No late-Gothic Revival church architect was as close to Pugin as Comper. Working in the Perpendicular style, the colour, scale, and pattern of the damask complements the beauty of the medieval work. The chasuble is a powerful symbol of the continuity of the Gothic style used as a valid architectural language and also links English medieval Catholicism with the Gothic Revival. Comper's death in 1960 coincided with the building of the Rhetoric Wing, the last Gothic Revival building at Stonyhurst.

In 2005 Gothic architecture reached a surprisingly undefeated conclusion in the new crossing tower of St Edmundsbury Cathedral in Suffolk, the most permanent of the Millennium Projects, designed by Warwick Pethers, a pupil of Stephen Dykes-Bower, and built of Barnack stone to last a thousand years. During the early course of building, Pethers was invited to Stonyhurst to talk about the cathedral and a lively group of pupils was enthused and surprised that such fine work was possible in modern times.

5.1

CONTRASTS
Augustus Welby Northmore Pugin (1812-1852)
(London, 1841)
Loaned by Heythrop College Library, University of London

Pugin was a prolific architect, but limited funds meant that few of the churches he built measured up to his own high standards. More significant in many ways than his buildings were his writings, and none more so than *Contrasts,* first published in 1836. It was a landmark in the progress of the nineteenth-century Gothic Revival.

Pugin did not favour the Gothic style merely on grounds of taste. For him, medieval architecture was *Christian* architecture, and Gothic was "not a style but a principle". *Contrasts* is based on the idea that buildings express the values and ideals of the society that produces them. In it, Pugin satirised what he saw as the meanness and immorality of his own age, reflected in its "pagan" neoclassical architecture and its use of "sham" materials. He contrasted this with what he believed to be the piety and virtue of the Middle Ages; and he did this largely through pictures rather than words.

In *Contrasted Residences for the Poor,* the medieval almshouses and dining hall attached to the church are the architectural expression of an ideal Christian community. It is an ideal echoed in nineteenth-century Gothic Revival building complexes such as St Francis Xavier's in Liverpool, and Stonyhurst, with their interlinked church, college and associated buildings.

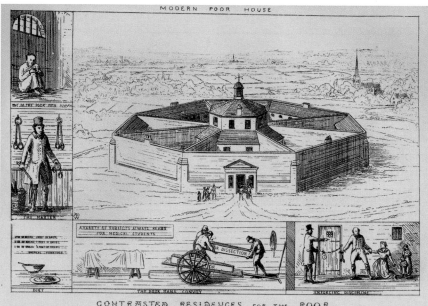

MODERN POOR HOUSE

CONTRASTED RESIDENCES FOR THE POOR

ANTIENT · POOR · HOYSE.

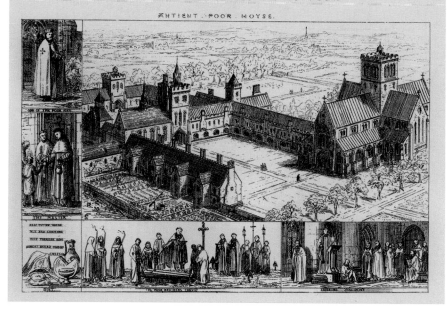

5.1

121

5.2

GLOSSARY OF ECCLESIASTICAL ORNAMENT AND COSTUME
Augustus Welby Northmore Pugin (1812-1852)
(London, 1846)

This illustrated dictionary of medieval design and religious symbolism is the most scholarly of Pugin's books. It is also the most sumptuous: the recently invented process of chromolithography is used for the illustrations, with lavish amounts of gold, so that it resembles a precious illuminated manuscript. The first edition published in 1844 was priced at six guineas; but, despite its cost, it was popular enough for further editions to follow in 1846 and 1868.

For Pugin, the medieval Catholic Church was the supreme inspirer and patron of art. The frontispiece to the *Glossary* represents his vision of an ideal church interior, beautified by Gothic art of every kind, from coloured statues, encaustic tiles and wrought metalwork to stained glass, embroidered vestments and mural paintings. The artist standing on a scaffold, putting the finishing touches to this dazzling ensemble, might be taken as a symbolic self-portrait of the book's author.

Pugin's idea of the re-created medieval church, expressed through books such as the *Glossary*, had an enormous influence on other nineteenth-century architects, as the decorative richness of churches such as St Francis Xavier's in Liverpool demonstrates. Pugin's belief that a building and its furnishings should combine to make a total work of art was central not just to the Gothic Revival, but to the Arts and Crafts movement that grew out of it.

5.2

5.3

FLORIATED ORNAMENT: A SERIES OF THIRTY-ONE DESIGNS
Augustus Welby Northmore Pugin (1812-1852)
(London, 1849)

Pugin intended *Floriated Ornament* to illustrate how modern Gothic design could – and should – be based on nature, not on the slavish copying of the art of the past. Despite this, he based its plates quite closely on a herbal published in Frankfurt in 1590. On each page are a variety of intricate, stylised patterns derived from particular plants and flowers, identified below by their Latin names. They are printed in bold, flat colours, without shadows or highlights, and they look very different from the naturalistic flowers that feature on mainstream Victorian wallpapers, carpets and other manufactured goods. Pugin said that his designs were suitable for stencilling on walls and ceilings, and this kind of decoration was indeed widely used in Victorian churches.

At St Francis Xavier's, Liverpool, the ceiling of the nave was painted in this way until it was reconstructed in 1948 following war damage. In the second half of the nineteenth century, other designers would develop Pugin's approach to pattern further, most famously William Morris (1834-1896), who used flower and plant forms as the starting point for his celebrated textiles and wallpapers.

1 Lilium Saracennicum. 2 Persoonia flexifolia. 3 Fuchsia gracilis. 4 Sotyrium triphyllon. 5 Lilium album 14?
6 Triorchis major mas. 7 Ribes trillorum. 8 Carduus lanceolatus. 9 Eryngium alpinum cæruleum.

5.3

INTERIOR OF ST FRANCIS XAVIER'S CHURCH, LIVERPOOL
Anthony Perry, English Heritage, 2003
Photograph by courtesy of English Heritage

With its pointed arches and traceried windows, St Francis Xavier's belongs firmly to the Gothic Revival, but it could not be mistaken for a genuine medieval church. Preaching and engaging the faithful in the liturgy are of central importance in the Jesuit tradition, so the architect Joseph John Scoles contrived to give the congregation of up to 2,000 worshippers a clear view of the altar and pulpit, making the nave very wide and dividing it from the aisles by the slenderest of columns in polished Drogheda limestone, unfortunately painted during the twentieth century. This is quite different from the typical arrangement of medieval Gothic churches, in which the altar is set within a deep chancel and is sometimes concealed behind a screen.

When St Francis Xavier's opened in 1848, the interior was relatively plain. Only gradually, as money became available from various benefactors, was it fitted out with the altars and other decorations that are the glory of the church today. The design of the high altar seems to have been a joint effort by Scoles and his pupil S.J. Nicholl – the documents are unclear – and was carved by the Liverpool sculptor, Edwin Stirling, in 1851. It was largely paid for by the Withnell family who lived in the parish and who had strong connections with Stonyhurst, three of their members subsequently becoming Jesuits. The pulpit, paid for by subscription from parishioners and other benefactors, was also added at this time; the great hanging crucifix, or rood, designed by Pugin's disciple, Thomas Earley of Dublin, was installed in 1866; and the inner and outer altar rails followed in 1887 and 1926.

The windows of the apse were plain at first, but stained glass was installed around the same time as the high altar. Bombing in the Second World War, however, destroyed this and the present windows by Hardman and Company date from the late 1940s. The biggest single change was the addition in 1885-7 of the magnificent Sodality Chapel, the entrance to which is visible on the right of this photograph. Designed by Edmund Kirby of Liverpool to accommodate a number of sodalities, or pious lay associations, it contains further richly decorated altars and much sculpture.

5.4

5.5

THE SODALITY CHAPEL, STONYHURST
Photograph by Roger Fenton
Albumen silver print, 1858

The sodality of Our Lady at Stonyhurst has a venerable history dating from its foundation at St Omers in 1609. It followed the founding of the first Jesuit sodality by Father John Leunis SJ (1532-1584) in the Roman College, after which the formation of sodalities in Jesuit schools was encouraged universally. The devotional life of the sodality consisted of reciting the Little Office of Our Lady and members were encouraged to carry out spiritual and corporal works of mercy. At St Omers the sodality also served both as a powerhouse for prayer for families in seventeenth-century England and Wales suffering difficulty and persecution, and as a repository for the many relics of Jesuit and earlier martyrs. Membership was not voluntary but was secured by invitation and election. It was reconstituted in 2005 in a modified form after a gap from the early 1970s when the Christian Life Community replaced it.

At Stonyhurst, the sodality met in the old Shireburn family chapel in the heart of the house from 1794 onwards. A new Sodality Chapel, built in 1856-9, was designed by Charles Alban Buckler (1824-1905) who was also responsible for lengthening it forty years later. Buckler was of the third generation of a distinguished Oxford dynasty of antiquarian Gothic architects and draughtsmen. Received into the Catholic Church in 1854, he was followed in 1855 by his three brothers who all became Dominicans. The Sodality Chapel was his first Catholic commission. Buckler was the Surrey Herald Extraordinary and the most scholarly architect of his generation. He designed the priory of Our Lady and St Dominic, Haverstock Hill, London (1874-83), and rebuilt Arundel Castle, in Sussex, for the 15th Duke of Norfolk in 1875-1900, the last great secular achievement of the Gothic Revival. In the Sodality Chapel the principal relics are of the boy martyr, St Gordianus, which were placed in a magnificent feretory of gilded wood, designed by Buckler, and set beneath the altar. It is one of the most delicate and elaborate examples of Catholic church furniture of the time.

Roger Fenton (1819-1869) was a leading English photographer of his day – the first war photographer, and the first to capture the image of royalty on camera. Born at Heywood in Lancashire, Fenton trained as a lawyer. In 1851, while visiting the Great Exhibition, he saw some of the earliest photographs made and was instantly

5.5

captivated by this emerging medium.

In 1855, Fenton was sent to the Crimea with the brief of taking images which would help reconcile the British public to an unpopular war. His memorable photographs were widely publicised and Fenton found himself to be a household name. He founded the Photographic Society of London (later the Royal Photographic Society, 1894) and was invited to Windsor Castle to photograph the royal family.

In 1858 he returned to Lancashire and photographed the Ribble and Hodder salmon pools, part of which lay on his land and part on the Stonyhurst College estate. He was invited into the College and took the earliest pictures of school interiors, including this image of the newly completed Sodality Chapel. His assistant was Father William Kay SJ (1831-1908), professor of physics at Stonyhurst, who had himself studied under the eminent physicist, Michael Faraday (1791-1867). Father Kay set up the first Stonyhurst Photographic Society and passed on the expertise he had gained from Fenton. Roger Fenton donated over one hundred photographs to Stonyhurst in gratitude for the free access he had been allowed. Fenton's work was the subject of a major exhibition at Tate Britain, London, in 2005.

DESIGN FOR STAINED GLASS WINDOW, SODALITY CHAPEL, STONYHURST
Charles Alban Buckler, *circa* **1860**
Pencil, watercolour and bodycolour on paper and canvas

This recently discovered design by John Hardman & Company of Birmingham, for part of the (liturgical) eastern stained glass window cycle in the Sodality Chapel, depicts an angel playing an organ. Hardman invariably designed the stained glass for Buckler's churches and secular work. Starting in the field of medieval metalwork, the Hardman manufactory rapidly expanded the scope of its production, supplying not only furnishings for churches (including the church at Stonyhurst), but also executing a great deal of work for the Houses of Parliament. Pugin trained Hardman's glaziers to execute his designs for stained glass. The firm went on to design their own glass, based on Pugin's principles, and this remained a key feature of their work for the next 150 years.

Stonyhurst also has a set of red Gothic Low Mass vestments designed by Pugin and executed under the supervision of Hardman's half-sister, Lucy (1793-1863), who was also the wife of his business partner, William Powell (1789-1861). In 1842 she established a workroom to deal with the ever-increasing commissions for vestments and other furnishings arising from Pugin's work. Her son, John Hardman Powell (1827-1895), who was Pugin's pupil, married Pugin's eldest daughter, Anne (1832–1897), at St Augustine's, Ramsgate, in 1850.

The first stained glass was not installed in the Sodality Chapel immediately on its completion in 1859, but appeared piecemeal over the following few years. The subjects treated in the stained glass of the chapel are connected with the life and virtues of Our Lady, who was the patron of the sodality, and particularly reflect the titles of Mary as recited in the Litany of Loreto. This was, and still is, recited at Stonyhurst College every Saturday evening according to the instruction laid down by Thomas Weld (1750-1810), the donor of the house and estate of Stonyhurst to the College.

Further stained glass was put into the chapel after it was lengthened, designed by Paul Woodroffe (1875-1954), an old boy of Stonyhurst, and a leading Arts and Crafts glass-painter, book designer and illustrator. The addition of these windows cast a better quality of diffused light, and the lengthening of the chapel brought the building to the size originally intended by Buckler and gained considerably in beauty of proportion. Woodroffe designed an appreciable amount of stained glass for Stonyhurst, notably heraldic glass in the boys' refectory, the lower gallery,

5.6

the staircase, and the Angels' Chapel; he also designed the bronze South African War Memorial.

5.7

DESIGN FOR ST FRANCIS XAVIER'S COLLEGE, LIVERPOOL
Architect, Henry Clutton. Illustration from **The Building News and Engineering Journal,**
19 May 1876, pp. 494-95, 430 x 335mm
Loaned by Professor Maurice Whitehead

By 1875, the number of pupils attending St Francis Xavier's College, Liverpool, had reached almost three hundred, making it the largest school in the English Province of the Society of Jesus. Bold plans were drawn up that year for a new, main building for the College, comprising a large central hall, capable of seating two thousand people, to be used for assemblies, dramatic productions and examinations, and a substantial range of classrooms to accommodate up to five hundred pupils.

Father Richard Vaughan SJ (1826-1899) – uncle of Herbert Vaughan, the then Bishop of Salford and future Cardinal Archbishop of Westminster – who had been responsible for designing certain additions to the buildings at Stonyhurst in the 1850s, was invited to draw up the plans for the new College building in Liverpool, to cost £7,000.

Within weeks of ground works beginning, the provincial superior of the English Jesuits, Father Peter Gallwey (1820-1906), visited the site and declared Vaughan's plain design to be "not worthy of the Society of Jesus". Instead, a London-based architect, Henry Clutton (1819-1893), who had travelled extensively in continental Europe to study architecture, and who had already successfully completed work elsewhere for the English Jesuits, was commissioned to produce a new design. Though based on Father Vaughan's ground plan, Clutton's design was intended to be more in harmony with Scoles's existing design for St Francis Xavier's Church, complementing the latter building.

Clutton had published in 1853 his *Remarks, with Illustrations, on the Domestic Architecture of France, from the Accession of Charles VI to the Demise of Louis XII* and it was this close study of medieval French architecture which, in part, helped inform his proposed, elaborate building in red brick and terra-cotta for the Jesuit college in Liverpool. The project cost £21,000 and its success attracted national acclaim. This led to Clutton being invited in 1876 to design the large new church of St Michael, at Ditton, near Liverpool, for the German Jesuits who had recently been expelled from their homeland as a result of the *Kulturkampf* agitation under Bismarck.

Though the exterior of the new St Francis Xavier's College building, completed for economy without its clock-tower and spire, may have been adjudged a success, the acoustics of its Great Hall proved disastrous – and, unfairly, the Hall was for many years

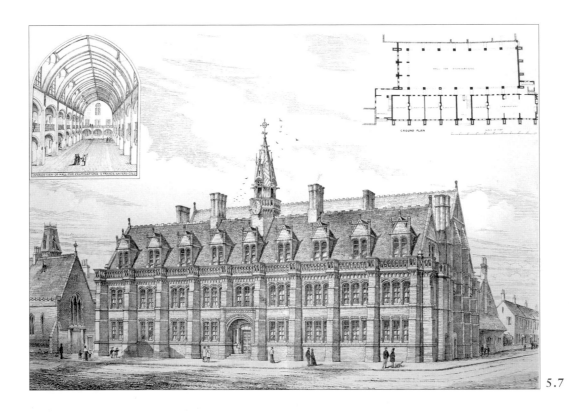

5.7

called *Vaughan's Folly.* Since the acquisition and £17.5 million pound refurbishment of the building by Liverpool Hope University in the past decade, the original cavernous volume of the Great Hall has been partitioned at the mezzanine level, creating an acoustically pleasing space now much frequented by the Royal Liverpool Philharmonic Orchestra and used also for an annual arts festival begun in 2000.

Appropriately, this fine Grade II listed building, which was abandoned and fell into serious dilapidation in the 1980s and 1990s, has been renamed *The Cornerstone,* recalling the words of the Old Testament psalmist: "the stone which the builders rejected is become the chief corner-stone" (Psalm 118: 22).

POEMS OF GERARD MANLEY HOPKINS: NOW FIRST PUBLISHED
(London, 1918)

The eldest of nine children, Gerard Manley Hopkins (1844-1889) was brought up in a moderately high Anglican family in Essex. In 1863, at Balliol College, Oxford, he met the poet Robert Bridges (1844-1930) who was to be a lifelong friend and who was to mentor Hopkins in his work as a poet. It was at Oxford also that Hopkins started his journey from the Anglican Church to Roman Catholicism, drawn to it not only by his reading of the early Church fathers, but also by an innate aesthetic sense of beauty that marked so much of his work. He was eventually received into the Catholic Church in 1867 by John Henry Newman (1801-1890), who was also an Oxford convert. Hopkins's parents were at first unhappy with his choice, but became reconciled to it over time.

Hopkins determined to take his journey further and become a priest, and, after agonising between following the example of St Benedict and becoming a monk, or that of St Ignatius and joining the Jesuits, he eventually chose the latter, starting his training in London, at Manresa House, Roehampton. Life as a Jesuit novice was simple and well regulated, divided between study, devotions and menial physical labour,

such as washing up, sweeping floors and haymaking. During his long training before ordination, Hopkins spent time at Stonyhurst where he greatly appreciated the beauty of the Ribblesdale countryside.

In 1879 he was sent as select preacher, or curate, to St Francis Xavier's in Liverpool. The parish was now enormous, comprising some ten thousand parishioners, of whom six or seven thousand came to Mass every Sunday. Immigration from Ireland by this time had so swelled the number of Liverpool Catholics that, domestically, many of the people were crammed together in close proximity in inadequate housing where disease and poverty made life very hard. The parish presbytery housed nine priests engaged in missionary work who divided between them the onerous task of caring for so many souls. Hopkins's own territory consisted of Jenkinson Street, Gomer Street, Back Queen Anne Street, Bidder Street, Birchfield Street and Bickerstaffe Street, all of which stood on the hillside just below St Francis Xavier's Church.

In addition to these duties, Hopkins was chaplain to the Brotherhood of St Vincent de Paul, whose task it was to visit and assist the very poorest households. His role as a

5.8

preacher was not a great success, and he felt the failure keenly. Sermons at St Francis Xavier's Church were famous throughout Liverpool and tickets would be sold in an attempt to restrict the numbers flocking to hear the more popular visiting preachers. Hopkins's preaching was too intellectual and many of the congregation considered his words to be cold and unemotional. He, in turn, felt unwelcome amongst the crowds of people to whom he had to minister, and he was unhappy with the frantic nature of his life which allowed little time for quiet contemplation and devotion. As he wrote to Robert Bridges:

> One is so fagged, so harried and gallied up and down. And the drunkards go on drinking and the filthy, as the Scripture says, are filthy still; human nature is so inveterate.

Hopkins wrote few poems in Liverpool. *Spring and Fall,* one of his most moving and well-loved, was written in September 1880, during a brief respite from the rigours of urban parish life, on a visit to Rose Hill at Lydiate, the rural home of the Lightbound family, nine miles north of Liverpool. The head of the family, Thomas Lightbound (1811-1895), a successful Liverpool flour dealer, was one of the nine lay men who had met at the *Rose and Crown* tavern in Liverpool in 1840 to set up a committee to build a Jesuit church in Liverpool. After converting to Catholicism in 1835,

Lightbound had married Catherine Lythgoe (1812-1875), the sister of Father Randal Lythgoe (1793-1855), the founder in 1842, during his time as provincial superior of the English Jesuits, of the Liverpool day school which had developed into St Francis Xavier's College. With the permission of the Catholic Bishop of Liverpool, the Lightbound family had a private chapel in their Lydiate home. There the Jesuits of St Francis Xavier's regularly went to celebrate Mass, often staying overnight at Rose Hill, enjoying both the country air and the company of the Lightbounds and their twelve children, the eighth of whom was Randal Lightbound (1851-1919).

The title of Hopkins's poem, *Felix Randal,* drew on his Liverpool pastoral experience – but with an echo, consciously or otherwise, of his recreational escapes to Lydiate. *Felix Randal* was written on the death of one of Hopkins's parishioners, a thirty-one-year-old farrier, Felix Spencer, from Birchfield Street, who died of a lung disease on 21 April 1880. Hopkins's depression at his surroundings and his work soon led to ill health and, in August 1881, he was moved to Glasgow prior to being sent to Roehampton.

Hopkins never returned to Liverpool, ending his working life in Dublin where he wrote the poems known as the *terrible sonnets,* in which he struggled with depression and despair. In 1889 he died in Dublin of typhoid. His last words on his deathbed were:

I am so happy, I am so happy.

After his death, Robert Bridges set about collecting Hopkins's manuscripts and the various poems he had sent to friends and publishers and, in 1918, he published this first collation of the work of Hopkins.

5.9

MANUSCRIPT COPY OF THE HABIT OF PERFECTION

Gerard Manley Hopkins SJ
Written in January 1866

Hopkins wrote poetry from his earliest years as a student at Oxford, but when he decided to become a Jesuit in 1868 he burned much of his work, considering that it was inappropriate for a priest to write poetry. Much of his early work survived, however, because he had sent copies to his friend Robert Bridges. This poem, *The Habit of Perfection,* survives in two manuscripts, of which this is the earlier version, originally entitled *The Kind Betrothal.* The poem published in 1918 is the later version, which differs slightly from this one.

When Hopkins wrote *The Habit of Perfection* in 1866, he was contemplating seriously his conversion to the Catholic faith, and the theme of the poem echoes that intention. It deals with the five senses which are to be subjugated in the desire for a deeper awareness of the transcendence of God, and the final verse suggests that the subject of the poem is a nun.

This manuscript was saved by Father Francis Bacon, an English Jesuit colleague of Hopkins, who transcribed much of his work. The note accompanying the manuscript suggests that he collected it after 1884 when Hopkins was in Dublin.

For his first seven years as a Jesuit, Hopkins wrote no poetry until, in 1875, the rector of St Beuno's College in north Wales, where Hopkins was on retreat, suggested he write something to commemorate the *Deutchsland,* a ship which had foundered in storms in December of that year with the loss, in desperate circumstances, of sixty passengers, five of whom were Franciscan nuns. A number of publishers rejected the lengthy and complicated poem as incomprehensible, but Hopkins felt free to write again. His poetry was revolutionary in its use of irregular and discordant sprung rhythm. His innate love of nature and his ability to see God in all things, which sprang from the words of St Ignatius, inspired some of his most famous poems. In 1975 Hopkins was honoured with a memorial plaque in Poets' Corner in Westminster Abbey.

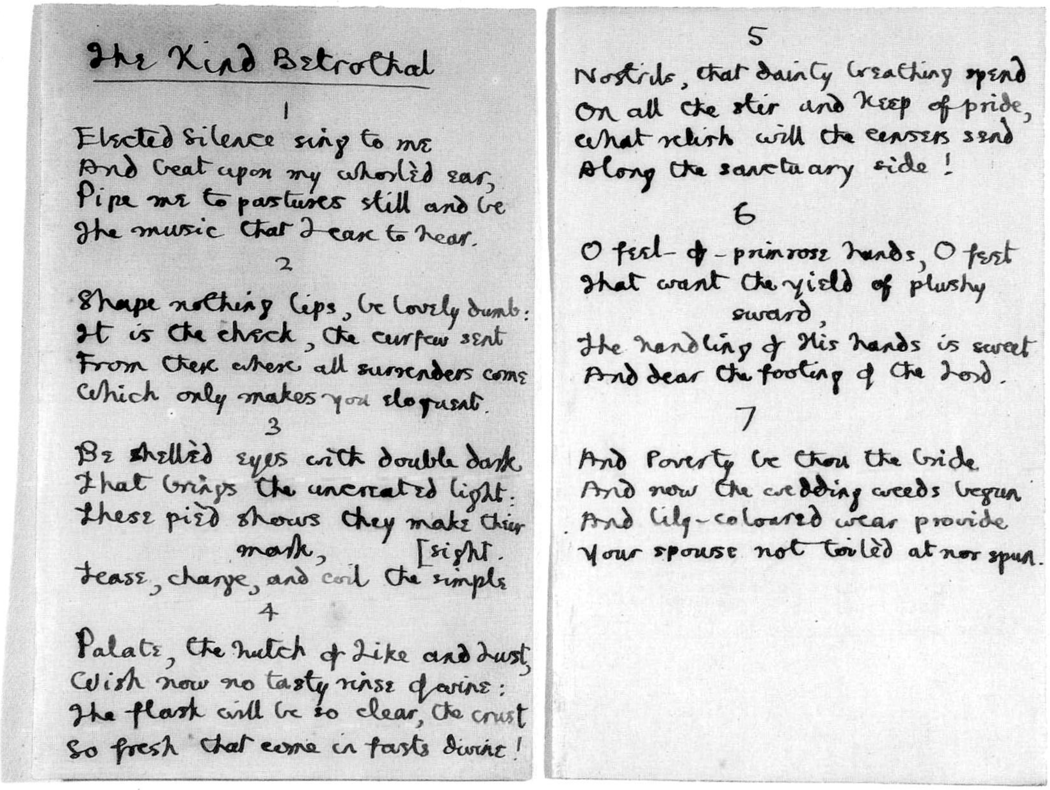

The Kind Betrothal

1

Elected Silence sing to me
And beat upon my whorlèd ear,
Pipe me to pastures still and be
The music that I care to hear.

2

Shape nothing lips, be lovely dumb:
It is the shut, the curfew sent
From there where all surrenders come
Which only makes you eloquent.

3

Be shellèd eyes with double dark
That brings the uncreated light.
These pied shows they make their mask,   [sight.
Tease, change, and coil the simple

4

Palate, the hutch of like and lust,
Wish now no tasty rinse of wine:
The flask will be so clear, the crust
So fresh that come in fasts divine!

5

Nostrils, that dainty breathing spend
On all the stir and keep of pride,
What relish will the censers send
Along the sanctuary side!

6

O feel-of-primrose hands, O feet
That want the yield of plushy
      sward,
The handling of His hands is sweet
And dear the footing of the Lord.

7

And Poverty be thou the bride
And now the wedding weeds begun
And lily-coloured wear provide
Your spouse not toilèd at nor spun.

5.9

5.10

THE BOYS' CHAPEL, STONYHURST COLLEGE
Published by J. Akerman of London
Lithograph 1888, 270 x 211mm

In 1878, the rector of Stonyhurst College, Father Edward Purbrick (1830-1914), launched an appeal to build a new chapel there in the Gothic style. As prospective benefactors were informed:

> The College numbers in its community more than twenty priests and sixty non priests. Each of the latter is bound to say special prayers and a Rosary every week for the Benefactors of the College; and weekly and monthly Masses to the number of four hundred a year will be said for the same intention.

The successful appeal, augmented by a massive personal donation from Father William Eyre, SJ (1823-1898), much to the disapproval of his brother, Charles Petre Eyre (1817-1902), then newly appointed Archbishop of Glasgow, led to the construction of one of the most beautiful chapels at the College.

Joseph Hansom (1803-1882), of the firm Dunn & Hansom, planned both the interior and the exterior. The chapel features spectacular fan vaulting, statues of Jesuit saints and martyrs and a glowing reredos telling the life story of the youthful Jesuit, St Aloysius Gonzaga (1568-1591), patron both of Catholic youth and of Stonyhurst College. The four paintings were designed by Hansom and executed by Percy Bacon.

The lithograph shows the proposed interior scheme in 1888, the year in which the building work was completed. The purpose of the print was to mark the end of the first phase – the construction of the exterior – and to raise consciousness (and funds) for the interior. So lavish and detailed was the decoration inside the chapel that it took until 1900 to complete.

DRAWN BY H.MONTGOMERY.   :The Chapel . Stonyhurst: DUNN HANSOM & DUNN. ARCHITECTS. 1888.

5.9

141

5.11
ST FRANCIS XAVIER'S, LIVERPOOL
Limited edition lithograph, by an unknown artist, 1892, 430 x 300mm
Loaned by Professor Maurice Whitehead

This lithograph was published in 1892 in a limited edition, of which this copy is numbered 333.

The rector of St Francis Xavier's, Father Thomas Murphy SJ (1838-1894), commissioned the drawing. It celebrated the golden jubilee in 1892 of the opening of St Francis Xavier's College – a school "to be conducted by masters from, and in connection with, Stonyhurst", as the original prospectus of 1842 had announced. The lithograph also celebrated the fact that, following the opening of the Sodality Chapel in 1887, the full *collegium* of St Francis Xavier was now complete in the manner envisaged by the lay committee which had resolved in 1840 to present a new church of St Francis Xavier to the president of Stonyhurst College.

The jubilee of 1892 attracted wide press attention. *The Birmingham Daily Post,* for example, was fascinated by the range and scope of the educational provision being offered by the Jesuits in Liverpool, as it informed its readers on 22 November 1892:

St Francis Xavier's College, Salisbury Street, Liverpool ... is the largest Jesuit establishment in the country. The area covered by the college, church, schools, and presbytery grounds is about two-and-a-half acres. Within this space is situated a centre of religious and educative influence of surprising extent, and second to none in these islands. The establishment is a complete, compact block of itself, standing aloof from all other buildings. The college externally is an imposing building, while internally it is very commodious and well adapted for its purpose. The elementary schools, which front Haigh Street, are probably the largest schools in England. There are about 2,000 children on the books.

Even by late Victorian standards of Christian religious observance, the high level of church attendance at St Francis Xavier's was worthy of particular comment:

The religious services each morning are numerously attended, and at the evening services, which take place every night, the attendance is frequently very large. The Sunday services commence with low masses at an early hour, and continue almost without interruption until eleven o'clock, when high mass begins, and ends the first portion of the sanctification of Sunday. In the afternoon there is a monster

congregation of children, and in the evening the Benediction service is again attended by a congregation which on some occasions runs up to 2,000 individuals.

The St Francis Xavier's College *Proclamation* ceremony, or annual distribution of prizes, held in December 1892, was presided over by the then newly elected Spanish superior general of the Society of Jesus, Father Luis Martín (1846-1906), who visited Liverpool specially for the jubilee celebrations. Martín took a particular interest in the educational work of the Society of Jesus and was concerned, from his wide international perspective, that Jesuit success in Liverpool was not yet being replicated in the capital city of the British empire. Earlier that year, he had already ordered the opening of a new Jesuit school in London – to become Wimbledon College in 1893 – and a second London school, St Ignatius' College, Stamford Hill, followed in 1894. In that same year, Father Martín raised the small Jesuit grammar school in Preston, founded in 1865, to the official status of a *collegium inchoatum,* or Jesuit *college-in-the-making:* it became Preston Catholic College in 1898. Finally, in 1896, Martín approved the foundation within the University of Oxford of a private house of study for members of the Society of Jesus, known today as Campion Hall.

The name of the artist who produced the 1892 jubilee lithograph is unknown. Curiously, the artist's proportions for the Sodality Chapel are totally out of scale with the rest of the buildings. Earlier depictions of continental European Jesuit colleges almost certainly influenced the commission of this late-nineteenth-century romanticised view of St Francis Xavier's. In its presentation of the full architectural extent of the college in Liverpool, the lithograph is particularly reminiscent of seventeenth-century engravings of colleges in the Flandro-Belgic province of the Society of Jesus, much reproduced in mainland Europe in the eighteenth century.

5.12

AERIAL VIEW OF ST FRANCIS XAVIER'S CHURCH, COLLEGE AND SCHOOLS
Photograph by A.W. Hobart, 1930
Liverpool Record Office, Liverpool Libraries, Small Prints and Photographs Collection:
Aerial Views 1930-39

When the foundation stone of St Francis Xavier's Church was laid in August 1842, the Everton district was one of the most salubrious and desirable suburbs of Liverpool in which to live. Its situation at the summit of a hill, on the edge of the town, surrounded by fields, with commanding views over the River Mersey, had already led, from 1825, to the development of fine ranges of merchants' houses which still survive today in Shaw Street. Everton was also the home of an emerging Anglican educational foundation, the Liverpool Collegiate Institution, begun in 1840 and completed in 1843, opposite the site on which the Jesuit church was then being built.

This aerial view of 1930 demonstrates how radically a once tranquil, semi-rural location had changed in the space of ninety years. Between 1800 and 1840, the population of Liverpool had grown from 80,000 inhabitants to over 286,000. During this time it had become Britain's principal Atlantic port, as well as the main distribution point for the cotton produced by the booming Lancashire cotton mills.

Further immense growth of the town, not least following the influx of 296,231 Irish emigrants through the port in the peak year of the Irish famine, 1847, altered the face of Liverpool completely, speeding up a process of urbanisation which was already well under way. Though many of those escaping the Irish famine moved across the north of England into other parts of Lancashire and Yorkshire, and though more than 134,000 of those Irish emigrants sailed on from Liverpool to North America in 1847 alone, many settled in Liverpool, swelling the existing Catholic population and creating a need for more churches and schools. By 1851, twenty per cent of the population was Irish. By 1861, Liverpool, with 463,000 inhabitants, was the second largest town in England and was duly raised to the status of a city in 1880. Between 1861 and 1931, the population of Liverpool had almost doubled to 856,000 inhabitants.

The photograph also reveals the full architectural extent of the missionary and educational outreach of the Jesuits in Liverpool in the early part of the twentieth century. Behind the long range of buildings in Salisbury Street *(from left to right, St Francis Xavier's Church, the large, thirty-eight-bedroom Jesuit residence and St Francis Xavier's College)* lie the parish elementary schools in Haigh Street and the two parochial schools, one for junior boys and another for pupils with exceptional talents, on either side of Langsdale Street, situated immediately behind and to the left of the church spire in the photograph. In the background can be seen the fine thirteen-bay battlemented Tudor Gothic façade of the Liverpool Collegiate Institution, designed by Harvey Lonsdale Elmes (1814-1847) soon after his success in the contests for the design of the St George's Hall and Assize Courts in Liverpool in 1839; and, to its left, the Anglican Church of St Augustine, of 1830, which was to be destroyed in the May blitz of 1941.

In the wider context of the Roman Catholic Church in England and Wales in 1930, the population of St Francis Xavier's parish was the largest, at 13,000; St Francis Xavier's College, with 680 pupils, was the largest Catholic secondary school; and the community of thirty Jesuits serving the college and parish in Liverpool was then the largest urban concentration of manpower in the English Province of the Society of Jesus.

Within the space of a few years, this picture was to change radically. In 1941 the Society of Jesus purchased a twenty-acre estate at High Lee in the Liverpool suburb of Woolton, with a view to the eventual, post-war relocation of St Francis Xavier's College to a more leafy and airy environment, with excellent sports facilities, away from the smoke and overcrowding of central Liverpool. While this aim was achieved with the best of intentions, the removal of the College to Woolton in 1961 effectively dislocated the combined missionary, educational and cultural basis on which the full *collegium* of St Francis Xavier had been conceived and carefully constructed in Liverpool over the previous century.

By the early 1960s, Liverpool itself was rapidly entering what were to prove several decades of serious economic decline. Changing patterns of world trade, the advent of transatlantic air travel and the disappearance from the skyline of majestic transatlantic liners, which for decades had plied between Liverpool and New York, and the disappearance of other commercial shipping which had connected Liverpool with a host of other ports world-wide for generations, brought with it a civic loss of confidence as the population of the city dwindled. More locally, during the 1950s and 1960s, the aftermath of the heavy bombardment in 1941 of the area around St Francis Xavier's Church, combined with the post-war relocation of much of the inner-city population to new housing developments in the Liverpool suburbs, seriously eroded the population of what, only a short time earlier, had been the most thriving of parishes.

By 1980, urban decay had so severely affected the area that plans were drawn up to demolish the nave of the church. These were fiercely resisted by a national campaign to save what was then described as "the most complete and moving repository of Victorian Catholic art" in Britain. Since that time, new houses have been built in the district and the

5.12

local community has started to regain some of its former confidence.

In 1997, Liverpool Hope University College took over the ownership of the buildings formerly occupied by St Francis Xavier's College and by the parish schools, helping the process of regeneration and injecting new life into the district by creating a cultural centre for drama, music and fine arts. St Francis Xavier's Church was re-roofed at this time at a cost of £980,000. Once this work was completed, the church reopened on 8 December 2001 with a service to mark the amalgamation of two local parishes – St Joseph's and St Mary of the Angels – with St Francis Xavier's to form a new parish. On this occasion, the Sodality Chapel of 1887 was renamed and a new chapter of parish life began.

Almost six years later, on 2 December 2007, the 300th anniversary of the arrival in Liverpool of Father William Gillibrand SJ (1716-1779), the first Catholic priest to take up residence in the town after the Reformation, was duly commemorated. The tercentenary was marked by the unveiling in the Sodality Chapel of a newly designed shrine to the Blessed Virgin Mary. This was dedicated under the medieval title of *St Mary del Quay*, the name of Liverpool's first chapel, situated on the banks of the Mersey in the early Middle Ages, close to the present-day Liverpool Parish Church of Our Lady and St Nicholas with St Anne.

Considerable work remains to be done to restore St Francis Xavier's Church to its full former splendour. The heating and electrical wiring systems were completely renewed in the spring of 2008. The powerful four-manual organ of 1907, by the noted organ builder, Hill of London, the largest such instrument in any Liverpool parish church, at present lies silent, awaiting restoration. Yet the fine peal of eight bells – a rarity in English Catholic churches – installed in the church tower in 1870, is again in full working order, following its restoration in 2005 at a cost of £19,000. This money was raised by the Liverpool Universities' Society of Change Ringers who enjoy regular use of the belfry, now their home tower.

Today working in close association with its neighbour, Liverpool Hope University, the only ecumenical university in Europe, and continuing to develop the close link with Stonyhurst College first established in 1840, St Francis Xavier's, Liverpool, with the support of the British Province of the Society of Jesus, continues its long tradition of missionary, educational and cultural outreach into the community.

THE WEST FRONT, STONYHURST COLLEGE

Photograph by Roger Fenton

Albumen silver print, 1858

Jesuit Missionaries – and God's Mission

MICHAEL BARNES SJ

Today the word *mission* has a very specific connotation for Christians. It conjures up images of distant outposts where envoys from the centre seek to establish a local Church. But it was only with the great colonial expansion of the sixteenth century, when a European Church travelled east and west in the wake of the colonial empires, that the word was used in this way. Before that, various terms were used to refer to the Church's missionary activity – *propagating the faith, preaching the Gospel* and *planting the Church. Mission* itself had a much more abstract theological sense – the sending of the Son and the Holy Spirit into the world by God the Father.

Jesuits understand this distinction. Today they speak of themselves as being *missioned* – receiving a charge from superiors. They are *sent* – a reminder that mission is an action before it is a thing. The practice began, of course, with St Ignatius Loyola. He was driven by a very simple yet powerful vision. Other religious orders had been named after their founder. Ignatius wanted his men to be companions of Jesus: Jesus alone was to be the centre of Jesuit life. Thus when the first Jesuits were *missioned*, they carried with them a deep sense of companionship with

Jesus and, in the Spirit of Christ, companionship with each other. Ignatius's spirituality, in other words, ensured that the early Jesuits never lost sight of that original theological meaning of the word *mission*. They knew they were co-operating with what is specifically *God's* work.

This may go some way towards explaining the imagination and creativity exhibited by the Jesuit missions which flourished up to the time of the suppression of the Society of Jesus in 1773. Jesuit formation encouraged discernment and initiative. The Jesuits were often highly intelligent men, schooled in the rigorous thinking of St Thomas Aquinas and the richness of Renaissance humanism. They were taught to adapt to local needs, to discern the leading of the Spirit, and to live out their contemplative vision of a world made alive by the loving action of God. The approach to mission which still sees Jesuits living like holy men in India, practising Zen Buddhism in Japan, running the Vatican observatory, or preaching the Gospel on MP3 players and websites, begins here. This is not to say that the early Jesuits had a well worked out missionary strategy. On the contrary, what was achieved emerged only from a sometimes painfully acquired practical wisdom.

The greatest example – the greatest missionary of them all – is St Francis Xavier – the patron of this church. He was born on 7 April 1506, the youngest son of a noble family in the Pyrenean kingdom of Navarre. His early years were happy and secure and he received a solid schooling. But, at the age of ten, his father, treasurer to the king, died and the family fortunes declined rapidly. Francis, a brilliant student, found himself at the University of Paris where in 1529 he shared a room with another impoverished nobleman – Ignatius of Loyola.

The group of companions who gathered round Ignatius became the Society of Jesus on 27 September 1540 when they received a formal seal of approval from Pope Paul III. They soon dispersed in response to specific requests. King John III of Portugal wanted Jesuits to support his rapidly expanding eastern empire. Ignatius's original choice fell ill. Xavier stepped into the breach and sailed from Lisbon on 7 April 1541.

In Goa, he quickly came up against the corruption and greed of Europeans stationed overseas. He worked at first among the poor and forgotten of the colony, the 'half-converts' whose baptism had been the price paid for food or clothing. In September 1542 he left for the southern coasts round Cape Comorin. He would go through the villages of the poor fisherfolk, ringing a bell. Once a crowd had assembled, he would explain the articles of the Creed, getting the people to use gestures, the sign of the cross, and to recite prayers

with him. Learning the Christian faith, he seems to be saying, is not a matter of blind assent but a process of moving the inner spirit, the heart.

It was not so straightforward elsewhere. In August 1544, he began a long period of four tireless years, working in various parts of what is now Malaysia and Indonesia. Here, Catholic missions were in competition with their Muslim counterparts. Xavier realised that it was only at the fringes of Muslim expansion that fertile mission fields could be established. Back in Goa in March 1548, a chance meeting with a young Japanese turned his thoughts to the Far East. On 15 August 1549 he landed at Kagoshima in southern Japan.

In Japan he found a very different religious world. After three years hard graft and a number of mistakes in translating his Christian message into the local vernacular, it became clear to Xavier that he would make no headway without first Christianising what he saw as the source of Far Eastern civilisation. Fascinated by the cultural unity of the Sino-Japanese world, he determined to enter China whatever the cost. He never made it. He got as far as the island of Changchuen, a couple of miles from the Chinese coast, where he fell ill in a small hut by the sea shore. Around midnight on 2 December 1552 he died. He was forty-six years old.

Xavier developed no theory of mission. He used interpreters, made do by picking up as much of the local language as he could, and – perhaps most important of all – taught people through prayer. Undoubtedly he impressed by the power of his personality. But he also learned how to adapt and to appreciate the wisdom of the culture which he encountered. The letters he wrote to Ignatius, sometimes taking years to arrive, became for his successors a rich source of motivation. A tradition, a particular style of missionary work had begun. Xavier's experience in Japan, of encountering a sophisticated people and learning how to engage with them on their terms, became the norm rather than the exception.

Several unsuccessful attempts were made to begin a Chinese mission in the years following Xavier's death. They failed, largely because of insufficient preparation. It was left to Alessandro Valignano, who arrived in Goa as visitor or superior of the eastern missions in 1574, to develop a proper training programme. For more than thirty years, until his death in 1606, Valignano exercised an extraordinary influence over the development of the missions. He insisted that his men should become not just competent in the local language but familiar with Chinese and Japanese culture and customs.

Valignano was aware of the political sensitivities surrounding the Jesuit missions in the Far East. It is significant that he and many of the men who came after him were Italian – and therefore not associated with the colonial interests of the Spanish and Portuguese. Jesuits like the extraordinary Matteo Ricci (1552-1610), who had been Valignano's novice in Rome back in 1571, had a freedom to experiment as they sought ways to adapt their teaching to the local culture. Without Valignano's trust and encouragement, it is doubtful whether the great Jesuit experiment in missionary accommodation – or *inculturation,* to give it its modern name – would ever have been possible.

Ricci arrived in Macao on 7 August 1582, and with Michele Ruggieri took up residence in Canton in September 1583. They began, rather in imitation of Xavier in Japan, by adopting the dress of Buddhist monks. This made perfect sense, especially as the Buddhism they encountered had many elements in common with Christianity. Only later did it become clear that the true source of Chinese culture lay not in Buddhism but in Confucianism.

This extraordinary experiment in accommodation between Christianity and Confucian social mores which Ricci began in China was not without its problems. Ricci argued that Confucian rites of 'ancestor worship' were merely a formal token of respect paid to the past. Converts were allowed to continue to participate in these rites. But what Ricci saw as legitimate adaptation to local customs, others regarded as pandering to superstition.

Support from Rome in the late sixteenth century had dwindled away by the end of the seventeenth. The so-called 'rites controversy' put an effective end to the independence of the

Jesuit mission. Jesuits remained in influential positions at the imperial court in Peking right up until the suppression of the Society of Jesus in 1773, by which time the number of native Christians was estimated at over 300,000.

A similar battle was fought by another Italian Jesuit, Roberto de Nobili (1577-1656), who arrived in India in 1605 and spent most of his life as a missionary in the city of Madurai. Like Ricci, he learned the language, studied Sanskrit sacred texts and started to live as a *sannyasi*, a high-caste holy man. This scandalised the established order of the Church. In his defence, de Nobili distinguished between what had religious and what had purely social significance – such as his wearing of the Brahmin sacred thread which made him personally acceptable to the Brahmin elite. De Nobili insisted that his method of adaptation was simply following the practice of the early Church. Most importantly, he emphasised that a precise situation was being addressed: these were the conditions under which the Gospel must be preached if Brahmins, the people of influence in the local culture, were to be converted to Christ.

In due course his principles became official Roman policy. In 1659 *Propaganda Fide* echoed de Nobili by stating unequivocally that European missionaries were to take with them not "France, Spain, or Italy or any part of Europe" but the Faith "which does not reject or damage any people's rites and customs, provided these are not depraved".

These are just the most familiar names. But there were many other remarkable Jesuits who took the message of the Gospel to distant parts and, through their scholarly and scientific work, made a lasting impact on the places they visited. One such was Ippolito Desideri who travelled over the Himalayas to Tibet, arriving in Lhasa on 18 March 1716. There he presented a book which he had written in Tibetan verse to the king, and set himself to master the subtleties of Tibetan Buddhism. His work shows a remarkable grasp of some of the most important Buddhist teachings, particularly the concept of 'no soul'. But his time in Lhasa was all too short. War intervened, the king was killed and Desideri was forced to leave the city. In 1721 he was recalled and Rome gave the mission area to the care of the Capuchins.

The missions of Asia are celebrated for scholarly theological engagement with a sophisticated religious culture, an engagement made possible by heroic individuals like Ricci and de Nobili deliberately choosing to work away from the centres of colonial power. In South America, Jesuit missionary work took on a much more political edge. This was because the celebrated reductions – so familiar to British film audiences from *The Mission*, starring Jeremy Irons and Robert de Niro – directly challenged the norms and assumptions on which missionary activity had largely been based.

The reductions covered large tracts of land in what is now northern Argentina, Paraguay, southern Brazil and Uruguay. In developing this extraordinary experiment in Christian living – in many ways a return to the social principles of primitive Christianity – the Jesuits were indebted to the work of the great Dominican missionary and theologian, Bartolomé de las Casas (1484-1556). Horrified by what he had witnessed at first hand in central and south America, Las Casas had written that there was only one way to preach the Gospel – the way of justice, in imitation of the way of Jesus himself. This unique experiment lasted nearly 150 years, from the first settlement in 1609 until the expulsion of the Society from the Portuguese empire in 1759 and from the Spanish empire in 1767.

The Jesuits' first concern was severely practical – to protect tribes like the Guaraní from rapacious slave-hunters and colonial administrators. But gradually small independent republics grew up, holding land in common, framing their own laws, founding schools, hospitals and free public services for the poor. While the Church and its regular round of liturgical prayer were always at the centre of each community, the Jesuits also encouraged local culture, sculpture and woodcarving, dance and music. This was *total* mission, with the whole of life evangelised – suffused with the spirit of the Gospel. While it is inevitable that the few ruins of these settlements which remain today evoke a certain romantic feel, there can be little doubt that the idealism and sheer practical good

sense of the Jesuits did produce something quite extraordinary.

These few examples must suffice to illustrate the great Jesuit experiment in Christian mission. Many more could be mentioned. From the initiatives of a few individual pioneers in South Asia and the Far East to the more corporate efforts of the South American reductions, Jesuits pursued the tasks to which they were committed with a single conviction – that this was essentially *God's mission*. The ambivalent relationship with the colonial powers, in many ways the fault-line which ran through these centuries, led to the tragedy of the suppression of the Society of Jesus in 1773. But when the Society was formally restored some forty years later, the same spirit of imaginative and discerning companionship with Jesus returned.

Like their early predecessors, today's Jesuits are involved in a vast spectrum of activities, from justice for refugees to dialogue with Muslims. The journeys may be shorter, the lines of communication easier to maintain, but there are still the political issues to be negotiated and religious and cultural frontiers to be explored. And, like their predecessors, Jesuits today rely on the Spirit of God who goes before them – living on their wits, learning from the world around them, adapting to circumstances, challenging the status quo and defending the oppressed. The particular forms may have changed, but Jesuit missionary effort is as lively, and just as controversial, as ever.

ILLUMINATED VERSES FROM THE KORAN
Vellum, pigments and gold leaf, 190 x 290mm
Tenth and seventeenth centuries

Calligraphy, or decorative handwriting, is considered one of the highest art forms in the Islamic world, because of the importance of recording the word of God.

Like much Islamic art, calligraphy is closely linked to geometry, using symmetry and mathematical forms for its artistic effect. The literal depiction of humans or animals is discouraged within Islam, as it is taught that the creation of living things is the province of God.

The inset verses in this manuscript are much older than the border. They are written in Kufic script on sheepskin vellum and reputedly date from the tenth century. The border was added some seven hundred years later.

The word *Koran* means *recitation* in Arabic, and is held by Muslims to be the words of God dictated to His Prophet Mohammed. The Koran is not thought to have been written down in its present form while the Prophet Mohammed was still living, but was collated from memory by his followers after his death.

These verses were presented to a Jesuit missionary in Persia in the mid-nineteenth century.

6.1

6.2

CHIMU POT IN THE FORM OF A GOURD AND A MAN IN A HEAD-DRESS
Black, glazed earthenware, 260 x 200 x 260mm
Circa 1100-1475

The Chimu culture predated that of the Incas of Peru, radiating out from the Trujillo valley in northern Peru, and lasting from the early twelfth century to the mid-fifteenth century. At the height of its power, the Chimu empire extended for over 1,000 kilometres. It was a powerful, aggressive military state with a centralised authoritarian government; much of its success as a civilisation was due to its ability to build and manage an efficient irrigation system. The Chimu lived in a harsh desert environment, and ready access to water gave them a wealthy and stable economy. Perhaps because of their struggle to mitigate the effects of an unforgiving sun, the Chimu worshipped the moon.

Around 1475 the Chimu were conquered by the Incas, led by Tupanqoi. The new Inca empire was to last only fifty years before it was overwhelmed by the Spanish conquistadores under the leadership of Francisco Pissaro. In 1532 Pissaro defeated the Incas and had their leader, Atahualpa, killed. Pissaro was attracted to Peru by the rumours of fabulous wealth and mineral resources. By 1542 the country had been subdued and the Spanish government declared it to be a viceroyalty under direct rule of the king. Over two hundred thousand Spaniards flocked to the new colonies during the fifty years that followed. The new settlers established sugar plantations and silver mines, using the *encomienda* system – ostensibly the right to employ the local population, but in reality a form of legalised slavery. Put to work in the mines and plantations, the native population of Peru fell from 1.3 million in 1570 to fewer than 600,000 by 1620.

The Jesuits arrived on the subcontinent around 1570, but were not able to set up missions until 1609. Their work in Peru and the neighbouring countries of Paraguay, Uruguay, Bolivia and Brazil was rooted in seeking a system of social justice for native peoples, and it reached its highest form in the reductions. These were organised communities based on the rules observed by the early Christians, with free access to education and health services, where people worked the land on behalf of all and the slavery remit was not allowed to run. Their antipathy to slavery and the success of the reductions led to political difficulties with the Spanish and Portuguese governments, and in the 1760s the Jesuits were expelled from South America, forced to leave their native communities to fend for themselves.

The Chimu were renowned for their

6.2

peculiar style of pottery, which was invariably fired a deep sooty black. This was achieved by restricting the oxygen in the kiln, which resulted in a darkened finished product. The pots were then polished to a glossy mirror-smooth finish. They took many forms, some startlingly explicit, often involving figures of humans or animals, and were mass produced using moulds. This pot depicts a Chimu man in full feathered headdress superimposed onto a gourd. It was part of a group of 75 similar examples presented to Stonyhurst College in 1877 by Juan de Yturregui who had been a pupil from 1874-6. Juan's family were prominent wealthy Peruvians. The original catalogue entry said that the pots had been taken from the tombs of the Incas.

6.3

WATERCOLOUR PORTRAIT OF FATHER MATTEO RICCI SJ (1552-1610)
Watercolour and body colour on paper, 670 x 490mm
Signed and dated January 1845, Charles Weld

China in the 1550s was a self-contained world with its own distinctive ancient culture. Since the eighth century, Christian missionaries had been trying to gain a foothold there without any real success. In 1552 St Francis Xavier died in sight of mainland China, without ever setting foot on Chinese soil.

That same year, Matteo Ricci was born in Italy. He became a Jesuit at the age of nineteen and six years later volunteered to become a missionary to China. Ricci was highly educated, having studied mathematics, astronomy, literature, philosophy and mechanics. On arriving in Macao he reported back to his superiors:

> I have applied myself to the Chinese tongue and can assure your reverence that it is a different thing from German or Greek ... the spoken tongue is prey to so many ambiguities that many sounds mean more than a thousand things ... as to the alphabet, it is a thing one would not believe in had one not seen and tried it as I have.

Ricci quickly adopted the dress and habits of the people around him, and became fluent in Mandarin. His intellect and wisdom earned him great respect in China, and it was his scientific expertise that finally won him an invitation to Beijing from the Ming emperor, Wan-li (1573-1620), who heard about his collection of European clocks. The emperor was greatly impressed with Ricci's learning and kept him at court for ten years, never actually meeting him, but his favour opened to the Jesuit the doors to Chinese society. Ricci lectured widely on physics, philosophy and Western science, attracting thousands to hear him. He died at the height of his fame in 1610, fully aware that he had achieved little in the way of converts to Christianity, but hoping that he had prepared the way for subsequent missionaries to build on his reputation. His epitaph read:

> The man from the distant west, renowned judge, author of famous books.

More than one thousand Jesuit missionaries were to follow him to China in the hundred years after his death.

This watercolour was made by Charles Weld, a pupil of Stonyhurst College in the early nineteenth century. He spent much time in Rome from 1845 to 1850 copying paintings of significance to the Jesuit order. An inscription by Charles Weld at the bottom of the paper records that the original painting hangs in the Museo Borgiano at the Collegio Propaganda Fide in Rome. It is assumed that the original painting was by a Jesuit lay brother living in China with Matteo Ricci.

6.3

6.4

BRASS AND SILVER CELESTIAL SPHERE
Brass with silver inlay, 400 x 250 x 250mm
Signed and dated 1623, Qaim Muhammed

This brass globe, which maps out the heavens for astronomers, is the eleventh oldest Islamic globe known to exist.

It was made in India at the court of the great Mughal emperor, Jahangir (1569-1627), whose son, Shah Jehan (1592-1666), built the Taj Mahal. Jahangir was a cultured man, keen on science, who welcomed western scholars and scientists, particularly Jesuit astronomers, to his court.

The globe is inscribed *Qaim Muhammed ibn Isa ibn Allahdad Asturlabi Lahuri Humayuni* and is dated the eighteenth year of the reign of Jahangir, 1623. The inscription identifies Qaim Muhammed as an astrolabe maker in Lahore. He was part of a remarkable family which had produced fine quality astronomical instruments for four generations. Their family firm was renowned for its celestial globes such as this one. The globe is seamless, made by a process known as the *lost wax method,* also used by western sculptors. It is likely that the globe was commissioned by Itiqad Khan, the brother of Jahangir's wife, Nur Jahan, and so was a highly prestigious object.

The principal stars of the heavens are indicated by silver dots inlaid into the brass and arranged in Islamicate zodiac form. The circle of the sun's path is clearly marked, as are the lines that divide the sphere into celestial longitude and latitude. The globe shows all the visible stars and the forty-eight constellations listed by the ancient astronomers such as Ptolemy. It is constructed in such a way that the observer has to imagine that he is placed in the heavens outside the constellations, while the earth is hidden inside the globe.

The faith of Islam requires its followers to pray five times a day at specified positions of the sun, and facing Mecca. Using spheres such as this one, astronomers were able to use the stars to define longitude and latitude, ensuring that they could pinpoint the correct location of Mecca and the exact times for prayer.

The sphere arrived at Stonyhurst by an unorthodox route, having been looted from the palace at Lucknow in 1858, following the Indian uprising of 1857, by an army officer, Raleigh Chichester, who then presented it to his old school.

6.4

6.5

IVORY VIATORIUM OF FATHER JOHANN ADAM SCHALL VON BELL (1591-1666)
Ivory and brass, 100 x 70 x 30mm
1638

Father Johann Adam Schall von Bell was a German Jesuit astronomer from Cologne who was sent to Peking (now Beijing) as a missionary in 1622. There, he was following in the footsteps of another famous learned Jesuit missionary, Father Matteo Ricci (1552-1610), and he was soon noticed by the emperor of China through his faultless predictions of the timings of two lunar eclipses. Schall wanted permission to preach Christianity to the Chinese, but for this he needed the emperor's approval.

As a test of his scientific skill, in 1627 the emperor ordered him to reform the Chinese calendar which was based on the movements of the constellations, and which over many centuries had become unreliable through inaccurate astronomical observations. Father Schall worked on the project until 1635, and the recalibrated calendar earned him great fame and respect, as well as the all-important permission to carry out his evangelising work.

Throughout his life, Schall was a respected and honoured scholar at the Chinese court, but on the death of his friend, the emperor, he was thrown into prison by jealous courtiers and condemned to death. He was saved by a terrible earthquake in Beijing which was seen as a judgement on the sentence on such a notable scholar. He was released from prison and spent the last year of his life in Beijing, dying in 1666.

The *Viatorium* was used for astronomical and surveying tasks. The lid of the case carries an inscription with Father Schall's name and the date 1638. The characters translate as *Sun and Moon dial for a hundred wanderings*. The circular brass plate on the lid shows the phases of the moon, and the twelve two-hour periods into which the Chinese day was divided. The dial shows the days of the month and the twenty-four solar periods of the year. Inside the box is a space which once contained a compass and a Chinese proverb advising the reader to be aware of the fleeting passage of time and of the need to use it wisely.

This instrument was the personal property of Father Schall, and it is a mystery as to how it ended up in a second-hand shop in Korea where Sir Walter Hillier, the British consul-general in Seoul, found it in 1890. He presented it to Stonyhurst in 1906.

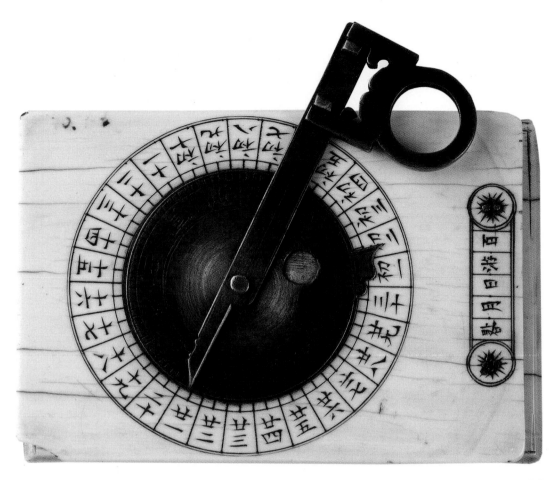

6.5

ST FRANCIS XAVIER AT PRAYER
Oil on wood panel, 720 x 530mm
Unknown artist after Peter Paul Rubens, *circa* 1650

Francis Xavier (1506-1552) was born in the Castle of Xavier in Navarre. At the age of nineteen, he travelled to Paris to study at the university, where he met Ignatius Loyola, and the two became companions, drawn together by their mutual desire to serve God. In 1537, Francis Xavier received holy orders, along with Ignatius, and worked for a while in Rome, helping to form the new Society of Jesus whose members were soon to be known as the Jesuits.

In 1540 King John of Portugal begged for the assistance of a Jesuit missionary to evangelise the people of the Portuguese East Indies. Francis left for India and landed at Goa in 1542. He spent five months preaching and caring for the sick, and became a familiar sight walking through the streets ringing a bell to summon the children to hear the word of God. Later that year, he set out for the Goanese pearl fisheries, where Christianity had almost died out owing to a lack of priests. He preached and travelled for five years in immense hardship, working in Sri Lanka, Malacca, and possibly even as far as Mindanao in the Philippines. He trained new missionaries and set up a noviciate to train new priests to minister to the people.

One of his Goanese converts was a penitent Japanese murderer whom Francis baptised *Pablo de Santa Fe*. His description of Japan filled the Jesuit with a burning desire to visit the country and to continue his work there. In 1549, Francis and Pablo landed at Kagoshima in Japan. Francis spent a whole year learning the language and translating the catechism into Japanese. His preaching met with resistance from local lords who banished him from the city, but he persevered, although with limited success. While in Japan, he heard much about China, and he began to plan his mission to the Chinese people.

In 1552 he set off for China, with only two companions. They stopped on the island of Sancian, just off the Chinese coast. Before he could achieve his aim of landing quietly on the mainland unobserved, Francis fell ill. He spent his last few days lying on the sands of the island, sheltered only by a rough canopy. He died within sight of China in December 1552 at the age of forty-six.

St Francis Xavier is generally considered as the greatest missionary since the time of the Apostles. In ten short years he travelled many thousands of miles to inhospitable and enclosed countries, and preached the Gospel. He set the standard for countless Jesuit missionaries who followed in his footsteps.

6.6

His practice and example of learning the local language and of adopting local customs contributed enormously to the success of later Jesuit missions. He was canonised with St Ignatius Loyola in 1622 and his feast is celebrated on 3 December.

6.7

MISSION BELL FROM THE JESUIT REDUCTIONS IN BRAZIL
Brass, 100 x 80 x 80mm
***Circa* 1700-1750**

The Jesuit missions or *reductions,* as they were known, located in Paraguay, Argentina, Uruguay and Brazil, were unique in missionary history.

South America was colonised by Spain and Portugal in the early sixteenth century, and, from 1609 onwards, the Jesuits set up missions for the indigenous Tupí and Guaraní peoples. In return for the promise of tributes, the people were to be exempt from the usual policy of *encomienda,* or forced labour, that prevailed in the rest of Spanish and Portuguese South America. The Jesuits also protected them from the slave traders of the region.

The reductions were run on lines that were based on the early Christian communities described in the Acts of the Apostles. The inhabitants worked communal land, and the produce of their labours was shared out equally – food and dress was the same for all. Free schools and hospitals were established in every community, and the Guaraní were reputed to be a completely literate society. They were skilled craftsmen and made intricate clocks and famously excellent musical instruments. Their working day was six hours long, as opposed to twelve or fourteen hours elsewhere in South America, and the remainder of the day was given over to music, dance and worship.

By the mid-eighteenth century there were a reputed 300,000 Indian Catholics in South America living on some thirty missions. In 1759 the Portuguese government, which had long regarded the Jesuits' work as an attack on their authority, passed a decree expelling them from their territories. In 1767 the Spanish crown followed suit. The Guaraní abandoned their havens and retreated to the rain forests in the years following the expulsion of the Jesuits. Today all that is left of one hundred and fifty years of a remarkable social and evangelical experiment is ruins.

The 1986 Roland Joffé film, *The Mission,* tells the story of the Jesuit expulsion and the futile war of protest fought by the Guaraní. The film is set in the mission of São Miguel das Missões, which is one possibility as the original home of this Mass bell. In 1894, the then provincial superior of the German Jesuit Province presented the bell to Stonyhurst.

6.7

6.8

JESUIT WARE PLATE
Porcelain, 200 x 200 x 30mm
Circa 1750

In the sixteenth and seventeenth centuries, Jesuit missionary priests took the Gospel teachings to India, Africa, Asia, the Far East and the Americas. Wherever they went, they tried to integrate local culture, practices and languages with the message of Christianity, and spent much time in learning to speak, eat, live and dress in the same manner as the communities in which they worked.

The Jesuit missionaries in China were quick to see the potential of porcelain manufacture as a vehicle for spreading the Gospel. By employing workers to paint on plates images from the life of Christ, they were able to reach a wider audience than they could by word of mouth alone. These plates were distributed all over China and many were imported back to Europe as *Jesuit ware*.

6.8

MODEL OF THE CHURCH OF THE HOLY SEPULCHRE, JERUSALEM
Wood, mother of pearl, bone and pigment, 400 x 610 x 420mm
Signed and dated Gioani Filio de Giuse de Gerusalemme 1760

The Church of the Holy Sepulchre in Jerusalem is built over the most sacred site for Christians – the rock of Calvary where Jesus was crucified. It also encompasses the tomb in which He was laid – the Holy Sepulchre – which gives the basilica its name. This is the place where St Helena, the mother of the fourth-century Roman emperor, Constantine, was reputed to have discovered the cross to which Christ was nailed.

After the failed Jewish revolt against Roman occupation in the year 70 AD, much of Jerusalem was destroyed and the site of the Crucifixion was hidden below a Temple of Venus. In 325 the emperor, Constantine, newly converted to Christianity, started to build a huge basilica, encompassing the Rock of Calvary, the site of the Tomb of Christ, and the place where his own mother, Helena, had found the Cross.

In the eighth century, Jerusalem was captured by the Persians and became a Muslim city. The rulers were generally happy to allow Christian pilgrimage to flourish, and the numbers making the dangerous and lengthy journey grew. In 1009 the Caliph was aggravated by the vast numbers of pilgrims and destroyed the church, hacking the site of the tomb down to the bedrock. The shock and outrage felt throughout Christian Europe was one of the catalysts for the Crusades which followed, starting in 1099. In the twelfth century, restoration of the ruined church began, and this continued down to the sixteenth century when much work was done by the Franciscans. Further work is still needed today, but agreement between the Christian guardians of the site of the Holy Sepulchre is difficult to obtain, and disagreements and tensions are common there.

Pilgrimages to this most holy of places have been taking place for almost two thousand years, bringing important revenue to the local inhabitants. People who made the journey in the past invariably wanted a tangible reminder of their efforts, and the souvenir trade has prospered in Jerusalem since the eighth-century German monk, Brother Felix, noted with dismay that the sellers of souvenirs followed him even into the church itself. That did not stop him buying many items.

This model of the church was at the top end of the market in souvenirs. It was aimed at the wealthy and fashionable pilgrim: it is made from expensively engraved mother of pearl and carved bone. The model comes apart to show the interior, including the Holy

Sepulchre itself. It was made in 1760 by an Italian craftsman, Gioani, whose father Giuse had evidently been in the same business and had gained some fame for himself as a maker of these models.

6.10
MODEL OF THE HEAD OF ST IGNATIUS LOYOLA (*circa* 1492-1556)
Silver, 290 x 20 x 150mm
Circa 1800, by Adamo Tadolini (?)

The first Jesuit church to be built was the *Chiesa del Gesù* in Rome. Work began on its construction in 1568 to the designs of the architect Giacomo Barozzi da Vignola (1507-1573), a pupil and successor of Michelangelo (1475-1564). The brief for Vignola was specific: the church had to be uncluttered, allowing the faithful a clear view of the altar where the Sacrament of the Eucharist was to be celebrated, and the acoustics had to be excellent, to allow the Gospel to be preached clearly and without confusion. Into this beautiful new church the leaders of the Society of Jesus placed some of their most important relics – the arm of St Francis Xavier (1506-1552) and the body of its founder, St Ignatius Loyola (*circa* 1492-1556).

The Chapel of St Ignatius, to the left of the main altar, was designed by a Jesuit, Brother Andrea Pozzo (1642-1709). It incorporated massive lapis lazuli columns flanking a colossal silver statue of the saint by the sculptor Pierre Legros (1666-1719). In 1797

Pope Pius VI seized the statue and had it melted down to help him pay war reparations demanded by Napoleon as part of the Treaty of Tolentino. A few years later a new statue was commissioned, most probably from Adamo Tadolini (1788-1868), who worked with the famous neo-classical sculptor, Antonio Canova (1757-1822).

The rector of the Gesù, Monsignor Ponzileoni, took the decision to encase the new statue entirely in silver so that it more closely resembled the Legros original. He first commissioned a chasuble and maniple made of silver and set with semi-precious stones, and then proceeded to have a silver head made. The head was made to life size, and when delivered it was discovered that it was too small for the larger than life body of the statue. The head was put to one side, and a new larger head was made for the statue. In 1870, the English Jesuit, Father George Lambert (1821-1882), secured permission to buy the head for Stonyhurst.

6.10

6.11

ARM ORNAMENT MADE FROM BEETLE WINGS
Plant fibres and beetle wing cases, 110 x 110 x 92mm
Circa **1800-1836**

This unusual, and probably rather uncomfortable, armlet comes from Guyana and was catalogued at Stonyhurst in 1836.

There is no information as to the donor, or the exact location in Guyana from which it comes, but it may well have originated with Charles Waterton *(see 6.19)* whose extensive collection of Guyanese artefacts remains at Stonyhurst College.

6.11

6.12

PAIR OF PLAINS INDIAN MOCCASINS
Deerskin, fabric and beads, 70 x 260 x 50mm
Circa 1850-1875

Much of early North American Jesuit missionary history is told through numerous letters known as the *Jesuit Relations*. In addition to relating the stories of such seventeenth-century Jesuit martyrs as Isaac Jogues (1607-1646) and Jean Brébeuf (1594-1649), they provide invaluable details of the customs and practices of the North American and Canadian indigenous people.

In the early nineteenth century the region from Saint Louis in Missouri to the Pacific Northwest was opened up by a Belgian Jesuit, Father Pierre de Smet (1801-1873) who arrived in America as a youthful missionary aged twenty. Following the trails laid out by fur traders and frontiersmen, de Smet travelled tirelessly, forming close bonds with many Indian people, for whom he was the one westerner they could trust. He defended them against exploitation and fraud at the hands of traders, settlers and government agents, and mediated between the government and warring groups of Indians.

For over twenty years de Smet worked for peace between the civil authorities and the Sioux Indians, and he was highly respected for his honesty and plain speaking by their chief Tatanka Iyotaka (1831-1890), better known as Sitting Bull. Father de Smet made no fewer than nineteen journeys back to Europe to seek support for the North American missions. On one of these European visits he travelled to Lancashire and spoke at Stonyhurst College.

Shortly after Father de Smet's death in 1873, an unknown Jesuit donated these deerskin moccasins to Stonyhurst.

6.12

6.13

BEADED ZULU ARTEFACTS
Leather, beads and plant fibres, various dimensions
Circa 1850-1890

This small group of beaded ornaments is part of a larger collection relating to the Zulu peoples brought back from Africa in 1893.

According to the original letters that came with the artefacts, they comprise a *Sinene*, or front part of a Zulu waist-band, and an *Ubusenge,* an arm or leg ornament. These were traditionally worn during courtship. The beaded gourd, which is lacking its stopper, is believed to have been used for snuff.

These objects featured in the 1923 Birmingham Missionary Exhibition organised by the Catholic Congress. This appears to have been an attempt by the Catholic authorities to raise consciousness, and, perhaps, also funds and volunteers for the work carried out by Catholic missionaries, both lay and ordained. The non-denominational evangelical London Missionary Society had held a very successful similar exhibition in 1908.

6.14

TABLETS DEPICTING THE INCARNATIONS OF VISHNU

Plaster, paint, gilt paint and varnish, 113 x 230 x 25mm
Circa 1850-1895

Vishnu is the second god in the Hindu *Trimurti*. The latter comprises three gods who are responsible for the creation, upkeep and destruction of the world. Vishnu is the preserver and protector of the universe. His role is to return to earth in troubled times and restore the balance of good and evil. Hindus believe that he has been reincarnated nine times so far, but that he will be reincarnated one last time to bring about the end of the world.

Vishnu is shown as having a human body, often with blue coloured skin, and four arms. In his hands he carries the conch, to represent the primeval sound of creation, the chakra, or discus, which represents the mind, the lotus flower for liberation, and the mace for mental and physical strength. He is usually represented either standing upright on a lotus flower with Lakshmi, his companion, near

him, or reclining in the coils of a serpent with Lakshmi massaging his feet.

These three tablets show both these representations of Vishnu, and were probably not originally meant for display in a box behind glass. They were collected by Edward Purbrick (1830-1914), an Oxford convert who became a Jesuit. Father Purbrick worked in England as rector of Stonyhurst (1869-1879), and as provincial superior of the English Jesuits (1880-1888), and he was later appointed provincial superior of the Maryland/New York Province (1897-1902). He was an inveterate collector of rare and beautiful objects, from sixteenth century altarpieces to artefacts such as this group of tablets. He sent many interesting artefacts to Stonyhurst as he wanted the pupils there to be aware of the wider world and its many peoples and cultures.

6.14

6.15 & 6.16
PHOTOGRAPH OF THE WESTERN WALL, JERUSALEM
PHOTOGRAPH OF THE GARDEN OF GETHSEMANE, JERUSALEM
Albumen silver prints, 287 x 243mm and 258 x 307mm respectively
Photographed in 1857 by James Robertson and Felice Beato

These two photographs are part of a collection of nearly 6,000 early photographic images collected by a former Stonyhurst pupil, Alexander Hill Gray (1837-1927), on his travels round Europe, Africa, the Holy Land, Asia and the Far East. Many of the photographs are from the most famous photographic studios of the day, but large numbers of them appear to be unique and may have been taken by Hill Gray himself.

Alexander Hill Gray was born in India of a Scottish family. During his six-month return voyage home, at the age of four, his mother converted to Catholicism and was consequently ostracised by her Presbyterian family. The Jesuits offered Alexander and his brother John a free education and, in 1842, he was sent to Stonyhurst. He greatly enjoyed his time at the College and retained a lifelong affection for the Jesuits.

In 1857 he joined the Sikh cavalry as an interpreter and witnessed the Indian uprising at first hand. On leaving the army, he spent much of his life travelling in some of the wildest and most remote parts of the world. He visited the Himalayas and Tibet long before other more famous travellers reached them, and roamed the Caspian Sea, Baku, Persia, South Africa (where he tried and failed to find Dr Livingstone) and on to Singapore and Borneo where he befriended a group of Dyak headhunters. In his last years in England he found new fame as a rose grower.

The Western Wall is the last remnant of the Holy Temple built by Solomon in the tenth century BC to hold the Ark of the Covenant entrusted to King David, his father. The Babylonians destroyed the Temple in 586 BC and the Second Temple was begun in 516 BC and expanded by Herod the Great (73 BC – 4 BC) in 19 BC. In 70 AD the Temple was destroyed by the Romans, leaving only the lowest seven rows of stones of the Western Wall standing as a warning to the Jews of the might of Rome. It is a place of pilgrimage and prayer, sacred to the Jewish faith, and venerated by Christians because of its associations with the life and Passion of Christ.

The Garden of Gethsemane takes its name from a Greek translation of the Aramaic words *gat shemanim*, meaning *oil press*. It is described by all four evangelists, who record that Jesus withdrew there to pray after the Last Supper for strength to face the sacrifice ahead of Him. He was arrested there and abandoned by His disciples.

The photographic partnership of James Robertson (1813-1888) and Felice Beato

6.15   6.16

(1833-1903) was highly important for the development of early photographic techniques. The two men went into partnership in 1853 when photography was still in its infancy and visited Jerusalem in 1857, taking these images amongst many others. Beato travelled on to India to photograph the Indian uprising, and may well have encountered Hill Gray there. His photographs of that conflict and of the later Second Opium War mark him out as the prototype of photojournalists, being, amongst other things, the first photographer to take an image of corpses on the field of battle.

6.17

GUITAR MADE FROM ARMADILLO SKIN

Armadillo skin, wood and catgut, 500 x 160 x 170mm
***Circa* 1870-1895**

This bizarre musical instrument comes from the Jesuit missions in Guyana. It is uncertain whether it was made to be used seriously or as a joke or souvenir. It was originally identified as being made from a coconut shell: possibly the cataloguer at Stonyhurst had never seen an armadillo before.

6.17

6.18

MARRIAGE CONTRACT BETWEEN ISMAT MEHSEPAN AND MIRZA ABDUL HUSSAN KHAN

Vellum, pigments and gold leaf, 299 x 378mm

1873

The first two-and-a-half pages of this Persian legal document quote extracts from the Koran.

The marriage contract itself authorises the Imam to join together the bride and groom in marriage and itemises a dowry of 6000 *tomans* to be paid by the bride's father to the husband.

The last two pages consist of twenty-four blank decorative medallions in which would be inscribed the names and dates of birth of the couple's children.

6.18

6.19

BEADED GARMENT OF THE PATAMONA INDIANS
Plant fibres, glass and shell beads, 500 x 300mm
Circa 1890

The Patamona people largely live in the highland forests of Guyana. Today it is estimated that there about 6,000 Patamona living chiefly as hunters and farmers in the more remote regions of that country.

Christopher Columbus was the first European reputed to have laid eyes on Guyana, in 1498. From the sixteenth century it became a busy Dutch trading post, with the new settlers initially happy to treat the original inhabitants as commercial partners. Relations, which began as cordial, soured as the Guyanese were exploited financially and then worsened into outright ill-treatment. Many Guyanese, such as the Patamona, moved up into the hills. To replace them as workers, the Dutch and British settlers brought in African slaves and, later, indentured Indian and Asian labourers to work their farms. In 1796 conflict between the Dutch and British governments over territorial sovereignty was ended and the British claimed Guyana as a colony for the crown. Guyana gained independence in 1966 and is today the only English-speaking country in South America.

The Jesuits who worked in Guyana from the mid-nineteenth century were mostly from the English (now British) Province. As missionaries, doctors, hospital workers and teachers, they established a strong foothold in the country, carrying out valuable work among the Amerindian population, who held them in high regard. The Jesuits founded and ran two hundred primary schools and three secondary schools, in addition to numerous mission stations.

This beaded garment or body ornament dates from the 1890s and is part of a significant collection of artefacts from Guyana held at Stonyhurst. These were acquired in part by Jesuit missionaries, but also by the explorer and naturalist Charles Waterton (1782-1865) who attended Stonyhurst as a pupil in 1795 and who owned estates in Guyana, visiting them regularly from 1811. Waterton is credited with discovering, during his time in Guyana, *curare* – a blackish-brown resinous bitter substance, extracted from various plants found in South America, and used by Indians to poison their arrows, and known by them as *wourali*. Waterton's scientific experiments with the substance helped to lay the foundations of modern anaesthetics. Indeed the correct technique for using curare in modern anaesthesia was developed in the 1960s by the Liverpool-born and Ampleforth-educated Thomas Cecil

Dress of the Indians of the
Patamona tribe, Guyana, given
by Fr John Gerard, S.J., in 1899.
('99 - 56)

6.19

Gray (1913-2008), Professor of Anaesthesia at the University of Liverpool from 1959 to 1976: it is today known widely as the *Liverpool technique*.

Waterton was a great champion of the Amerindian peoples of Guyana and used his fame as a scientist and naturalist to plead their cause, although his case was often undermined by his numerous eccentricities. In 1817 he visited the Vatican to ask Pope Pius VII (1740-1823) to intercede on behalf of the Patamona, but, unfortunately, while waiting for his audience, he became bored and proceeded to climb to the top of the dome of St Peters, leaving his gloves stuck on the lightning conductor. The pope was not amused and made him bring them down, and the subsequent audience was less than successful.

Contributors

MICHAEL BARNES is a priest of the British Province of the Society of Jesus. He teaches inter-religious relations at Heythrop College in the University of London and runs a small dialogue centre in Southall, a strongly multi-cultural part of West London.

LEO GOOCH has published widely in the field of English Catholic history. He is Honorary Secretary of the Catholic Record Society, editor of *Northern Catholic History* and author of *The Desperate Faction?: The Jacobites of North-East England, 1688-1745.*

JANET GRAFFIUS graduated in Fine Arts at the University of St Andrews and has worked as a curator at Glasgow Art Gallery, the British Council Art Collection, Guildhall Art Gallery, the Geffrye Museum and the National Trust at Ham House. She has been curator at Stonyhurst College since 2001.

JOHN ANTHONY HILTON is the editor of *North West Catholic History*. He has had articles published in *Recusant History, Northern History, Northern Catholic History, Midland Catholic History,* and the *Ruskin Review and Bulletin*. His books include *Catholic Lancashire: From Reformation to Renewal 1559-1991,* and his most recent work is *The Artifice of Eternity: The Byzantine-Romanesque Revival in Catholic Lancashire.*

THOMAS M. MCCOOG is a priest of the Maryland Province of the Society of Jesus, archivist of the British Province of the Society of Jesus, director of publications at the Jesuit Historical Institute in Rome and editor of *Archivum Historicum Societatus Iesu*. He has written extensively on English Jesuits in the sixteenth and seventeenth centuries.

ANTHONY SYMONDSON is a priest of the British Province of the Society of Jesus and a writer, architectural historian and conservationist. He taught at Stonyhurst College, Lancashire, and was curator of the college collections. In 2006 he published, in association with Stephen Bucknall, *Sir Ninian Comper: an Introduction and Gazetteer*. He serves on the Westminster Cathedral Art and Architecture Committee and is the representative of the Joint

Committee of the National Amenity Societies on the Catholic Southern Historic Churches Committee. He is currently completing a study of the church architect Stephen Dykes-Bower and a biography of Comper.

NORMAN TANNER is a priest of the British Province of the Society of Jesus. For long he was at Oxford University, as Senior Tutor of Campion Hall and University Research Lecturer in Church History. Since 2003 he has been Professor of Church History at the Gregorian University, Rome. He was editor of *Decrees of the Ecumenical Councils* (2 vols., 1990) and has written widely on church history. His next book, *The Church in the Later Middle Ages,* is to be published by I.B. Tauris in the summer of 2008.

MAURICE WHITEHEAD is a professor of history and associate dean of the Postgraduate Research Faculty at Swansea University. During his education at St Francis Xavier's College, Liverpool, study of his Lancashire recusant and Jacobite roots first awakened his passion for history. He is a member of the Council of the Catholic Record Society (CRS) and academic organiser of the 2008 CRS annual conference held in Liverpool. He has published widely on Jesuit educational history and culture.

DEBORAH YOUNGS is a lecturer in medieval history at Swansea University. Her research interests span the fourteenth to the early sixteenth centuries and focus on two key areas: the culture of England's gentry, and perceptions of ageing in medieval Europe. Among her publications are studies on the religious beliefs and literary networks of the gentry, and the recently published *The life-cycle in Western Europe c.1300-c.1500* (Manchester University Press, 2006). Her latest book, on the Cheshire gentleman, Humphrey Newton (1466-1536), was published by Boydell and Brewer in July 2008.

List of exhibits

The collegiate environments in which artefacts have been held in trust at Stonyhurst and at St Francis Xavier's, Liverpool, were strengthened over the years by official grants of arms which underlined the continental European links of both institutions.

Coat of arms of Stonyhurst College
Quarterly argent and vert, in first and fourth quarters a lion rampant guardant, and in the second and third quarters an eagle displayed, wings inverted, counterchanged, all within a bordure engrailed gules charged with eight patriarchal crosses of the first.

The arms of Stonyhurst College reflect its peripatetic history. The green lion is taken from the arms of the Shireburn family and the silver eagle from those of the Bayley family, the original owners of Stonyhurst Hall. In 1373, Richard Bayley of Stonyhurst married Margaret Shireburn and combined their arms, although, unusually, her arms appear in the quarters usually reserved for the husband's. She was a substantial heiress, which may account for the anomaly. The unicorn was the family crest of the Shireburn family, and the blue collar with the crescents added to the College arms refers to the Weld family, cousins of the Shireburns, who inherited the house in the eighteenth century. In 1794, Thomas Weld gave the suppressed Jesuits of Liège the use of his northern seat as a new home for the displaced St Omers College which had migrated to Bruges in 1762 and then to Liège in 1773. The red border and silver crosses bordering the shield are taken from the arms of the town of Saint-Omer, while the motto, *Quant Je Puis* meaning *As Much as I Can*, is taken from the Shireburn family crest.

The arms were granted by the College of Heralds on 28 December 1953. This may be seen as something of an afterthought for a school which was, by then, already three hundred and sixty years old, but it was perhaps considered that a College which had been founded in the reign of the first Queen Elizabeth ought to mark the beginning of the reign of the second Queen Elizabeth.

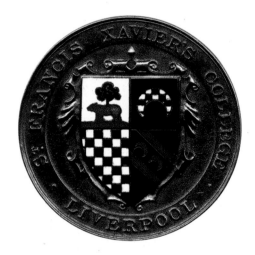

Coat of arms of St Francis Xavier's College, Liverpool
Quarterly; first – argent, a bear statant at the foot of an oak tree, proper, for Jaso; second – gules, a crescent inverted checky argent and sable, for Aznáres; third – checky argent and sable, for Azpilcueta; fourth – azure between two bends Or as many crescents inverted of the second, for Atondo.

In the early 1930s, the Duque de Villahermosa, a collateral descendant of the family of St Francis Xavier, granted permission to St Francis Xavier's College, Liverpool, to adopt and use the family coat of arms. This grant was duly confirmed by the College of Heralds in London on 23 October 1931.

Francisco Javier or, in Basque, *Xavier* (1506-1556), was born at the castle of Xavier in Navarre as *Francisco Jaso y Azpilcueta*, the son of Juan de Jaso and of María de Azpilcueta, who was the sole heiress of the aristocratic families of Azpilcueta and Aznáres. Francisco was given the surname of his birthplace. The four quarters of the arms depicted represent the families of Jaso *(top left)* – that of the saint's father; Aznáres *(top right)* – that of his mother's mother; Azpilcueta *(bottom left)* – that of his mother's father; and Atondo *(bottom right)* – that of his father's mother. The *gules*, or red, background of the second quarter of the crest, depicting the inverted crescent of the house of Aznáres, was adopted as the official colour of St Francis Xavier's College: that colour, and the Xavier arms, together subsequently became part of the distinctive uniform of pupils of the College, now a familiar sight in the Liverpool area.